Grace Fiddler

Ian Anderson
HERE COME THE REGULARS

Ian Anderson fronts the indie-pop band One for the Team, founded
the Minneapolis-based record label Afternoon Records, and is the
editor of the music blog MFR.

D0026927

Here Come the Regulars

Here Come the Regulars

How to Run a Record Label

on a Shoestring Budget

Ian Anderson

Faber and Faber, Inc.

An affiliate of Farrar, Straus and Giroux

New York

Faber and Faber, Inc.
An affiliate of Farrar, Straus and Giroux
18 West 18th Street, New York 10011

Distributed in Canada by D&M Publishers, Inc.
Printed in the United States of America
First edition, 2009

Grateful acknowledgment is made for permission to reprint the following material: excerpt from "Does Chatter Matter? The Impact of User-generated Content on Music Sales," by Vasant Dhar and Elaine Chang; the mission statement of Eclectone Records; the mission statement of Goodnight Records; the Militia Group one-sheet on page 115; and the Vitriol Independent Promotions one-sheet on page 117.

Library of Congress Cataloging-in-Publication Data
Anderson, Ian, 1985–
    Here come the regulars : how to run a record label on a shoestring budget /
Ian Anderson.— 1st ed.
        p.   cm.
    ISBN-13: 978-0-86547-981-4 (pbk. : alk. paper)
    ISBN-10: 0-86547-981-X (pbk. : alk. paper)
    1. Sound recording industry—Vocational guidance.   2. Sound recordings—
Marketing.   I. Title.

ML3790 .A626 2009
384—dc22

                                                            2009007985

Designed by Jonathan D. Lippincott

www.fsgbooks.com

10   9   8   7   6   5   4   3   2   1

I would like to thank my colleagues, family, and friends for their support and for encouraging me to write this book, which I dedicate to the young minds that will shape the future of the music industry

Contents

Here Come the Regulars

1

Getting Started

Some may say that I have no business writing a book about the music industry, and in a way, they would be correct. I'm too young to claim that I know much (let alone everything there is to know) about the business, because I simply haven't encountered it all just yet. But what I do have is the unique, generally unjaded perspective of a twenty-three-year-old, plus a lot of answers for those of you who are either just beginning to get on your feet in this industry or are getting your own label up and running. In short, I know the basics. I know what it takes to build a strong and healthy foundation underneath a business or a label within this often unforgiving and rarely welcoming industry.

Every record label is looking for their own Nirvana, Pavement, or Death Cab for Cutie. Breaking a band from obscurity to ubiquity and finding the next big thing that will change the world (or at least sell records) is what this business is all about. However, such artists are rare, and you can't wait until you find that next big thing to keep yourself afloat. Your label's survival depends on figuring out how to be successful without needing to actually be *that* successful. The old major-label model (or old joke, in some circles) is that for every blockbuster pop-sensation album, the label releases ten disasters that completely flop. One winner can pay for the other ten. But you may never find that megascale winner, so you need to learn how to build a label that can survive on scraps and sleepless nights, because that's what you'll have a lot of. The good news is that you can. It's possible to build a label that doesn't need a million-selling album. It's possible to build a label that can overcome your recoupable debt without sinking. It's possible to build a label that is smart, thrifty, and responsible—and that's what you have to be in order to stay productive and rake in some revenue.

I started Afternoon Records with a few close friends when I was eighteen years old. None of us thought it would turn into a career. Instead, we saw it as a good excuse to get together, listen to some records, and eat pizza. From there, it somehow turned into something a lot bigger and touched more people than I would ever have imagined. With a lot of work and a lot of love, it blossomed into the active little indie label it is today.

Beyond that, the meaning of the term *independent* is evolving as indie labels are becoming almost as big as the majors in terms of cultural influence, fame, and even record sales. More and more often, independent label sales break into the Billboard Top 100 in their first week (with such bands as the Hold Steady, Arcade Fire, or the Shins, for example). The grassroots followings these bands developed over years of touring laid a foundation for sales that competes with the biggest bands and labels out there. So being "indie" doesn't necessarily mean "small potatoes."

Being an independent label means that you exist to release the music you love to the world, whether it be pop-punk (which sells a lot of records), noise (which customarily does not), or hip-hop (which always outsells every other genre out there). What matters to an independent label is the passion behind it. We've all heard the old adage "You are what you eat." As a label, you are what you release. So it's important to put out music that you truly believe in and want to be a part of.

As an indie label, you are visible in your community. You may even become visible regionally or nationally. Fans can find you at shows, onstage, or at the local record store. You can be reached. And that accessibility is what makes independent music exciting.

Independent labels break down that fourth wall. We let people in. To be a success, a label doesn't need to be big in the *whole* world, it just needs to be big in its *own* world.

The music industry is an ever changing beast, so pay attention. We're always entering uncharted territory in this industry. Everything that worked yesterday is less successful today, and may even be less useful tomorrow.

We can thank John, Paul, George, and Ringo for this. Back in the 1960s, the Beatles set the bar for success at a dizzying height, and that bar is what the industry has used ever since as a business model. But there aren't Beatle-size stars anymore, and that model of doing business doesn't translate to today.

Today's music fans don't buy music, listen to music, or share music the way our parents and their parents did. Big music companies are struggling to appeal to us while they simultaneously struggle to dictate how we acquire and use music—and neither effort is hitting the mark or producing great results.

This is where independent labels come in. We are both fans and producers. We tend to believe that music should be available to (and possibly made by) everyone. New ways of producing, selling, and sharing music are less scary to us than they are to the big labels. Those very ways that threaten how big labels do business, give us the cracks in the door we need to squeeze into the industry.

Our generation, like those before it, uses music as a way of connecting with one another. On our social networking sites, fans connect with artists and the artists talk back to fans. Communities form around musicians and labels—and that kind of community identity is just one route to success as a label. But I'm getting ahead of myself.

The first thing you need to do is find your own label niche. Pinpoint where your label might be most useful. What kind of music drives you? What do you love? In your opinion, what isn't out there right now? What is your vision? Find your niche and build a fan community, and you'll earn the commitment of your artists.

Once you know your market and target demographic, then you've got to stick to it. Don't put out a metal record and market it to country listeners. I know it sounds obvious, but I've seen it happen. Try not to fall in love with a band that isn't right for you.

However, if you do, consider this: You can subdivide your label into minilabels that specialize in different genres. You can break up your services into separate sister companies: labels, publicity arms, booking agents, etc. You can offer all those services to your signed artists, and contract with outside artists on a service-by-service basis.

Here's a little more advice. Don't bite off more than you can chew. Yes, your parents told you that about course work back in school. And guess what? They were right. The same principle resounds throughout most aspects of running a label. Have fun and don't force it. If you have just started a record label, you don't need to manufacture ten thousand CDs, get them on shelves in Target, or make a music video for MTV2. Let things grow organically.

The best we can do as entrepreneurs within this industry is to maintain a certain level of flexibility and foster a willingness to explore the unknown. We must learn to walk blindly into the dark with our hands outstretched in front of us without fear, even embracing the knowledge that at some point we will most likely fall on our faces. That's just what happens in an industry as volatile, fickle, and unforgiving as the one we have chosen. I love music. It is a part of me. It is so integral to my life that I must always be close to it. Hopefully you feel something like this too. It's the only way we can justify being crazy enough to keep pushing. So if we're going to be in this industry, let's figure out how to survive. Together.

2

Your Team of Advisers

One of the mile markers of any college-level music business course is Donald S. Passman's *All You Need to Know About the Music Business*. Part one of the widely used music manual begins with this sentence: "Let's talk about the professionals you're going to use to maximize your career and net worth." Passman then continues to discuss the importance of a personal manager, an attorney, a business manager, an agency, and groupies.

Unfortunately, this is not the way things work anymore when you're just starting out. At the beginning of the long journey to the middle of this industry, help may never come to you. I know that sucks, but it's the truth.

You must learn how to become your own manager, your own attorney, your own business manager, and your own one-person agency. These things will not be handed to you, they will not be found or accessed easily, and, for the most part, that's really okay.

It's okay because we don't need all this extra baggage to do what we love. The music industry is, in one way, much smaller now than it used to be; fewer corporations at the top own most of the labels. But in another way, the industry is much bigger, because any average music fan–entrepreneur can accomplish just as much as a corporate team—with a little research, platform building, and constant phone calls and e-mailing, that is.

Right now, you don't need a manager. I don't need a manager.

We don't need managers. If you ever truly need the help of a manager, you'll know it: you will have double-booked yourself for a flight and a meeting at the same time while simultaneously forgetting to pay your utility bills because you just ran out of time before racing to the airport. You can look forward to that day, but right now, you must learn how to do everything—and all the legwork that comes with that everything—yourself.

You may never have a team of advisers, so you need to learn how to go it alone without that support system. Maybe someday you'll get that, but for now, let's prepare for the worst-case scenario. Hey, we're independent, right?

And now for those groupies. There's an outdated term for you. Indies don't need "groupies"; instead, we rely on fans and supporters. Fan communities are what indie labels are built on, and creating fan communities is what indie labels are also, happily, really good at.

Business Philosophy

Passman also offers a "Business Philosophy," four points to keep in mind as a music business person moves forward in his or her career. His first point is, "You are a business." No argument there, but I do have one with his reasoning. He argues that "you're capable of generating multimillions of dollars per year, and thus must think of yourself as a business."

In fact, you shouldn't think of yourself as a business because you'll make millions a year, because you probably won't. You should think of yourself as a business because not doing so cheats your artists out of professional support. If you think of your label as merely a hobby, your artists become a part of a hobby, not a business. Get it? If I were in a killer band, I would much rather have the benefits of being on the roster of a serious label than being attached to a weekend-afternoon project designed to fill a friend's spare time.

Think about it this way. If you're even considering starting a label, you are already serious about the music you love and want to support. You will have fun running a label, but honor your energy and effort by treating it as a business. Just the term *business* implies a level of seriousness that sets you apart from those who have a passing interest in music. So go ahead and use it.

What are the basic building blocks of a business? Make product, sell product; make more product, sell more product. See? You're a business the moment you a make a record and sell it for ten dollars at a local record store.

Let's take a look at Passman's second point: "Most artists don't like business." This is a great point, and you can make it work for you when you recruit artists. You've heard it said, "Those who can't do, teach. And those who can't teach, teach gym." It's the same for the world of music—sort of. Artists can create any number of varieties of music but may simply never be able to lock down the business end. On the other hand, some music lovers cannot create music but are wizards behind the helm of a business model. Artists who can't do business hire a label. And people who can't create art start labels in order to work for those who can. And those who cannot do either, teach gym. (For the record, I taught gym to kindergartners when I was a junior in college; it was probably the best semester of my life.)

In short, we exist to help. We are here to support artists and make their lives easier and simpler so that they can focus on what is truly important and what they are truly good at: creating music. No matter whether or not an artist likes business, their time is better spent in the studio recording or in their practice space writing, not worrying about mechanical royalties or digital distribution.

Passman's third point is, "Success hides a multitude of sins." He makes a vague reference to illicit drug use and unwise spending, but there's a bigger lesson here that I would emphasize more strongly. That lesson is, Don't be stupid. Don't stretch yourself beyond your means (either time-wise or financially). Don't rent a fancy office before you have the income to justify its fanciness. Don't say you can do more than you really can. Don't gossip about the business. Keep your head on straight, keep things in perspective, and try to be positive. It'll get you in less trouble and it will be more fun anyway.

Last, Passman makes this point: "Your career is going to have a limited run . . . the road is strewn with carcasses of aging rock stars who work for rent money on nostalgia tours. So take the concentrated earnings of a few years and spread them over a forty-five-year period." Well, let's be honest. Getting the rent paid means doing pretty well, in my opinion. That's the one thing you really have to worry about. That, and maybe health insurance.

3

Branding and Beyond

Branding is a business term that simply means knowing who you are and working hard to help people perceive you exactly that way.

First, you have to know yourself well. Make a list of points that describe who you are and what your label is, who your fans are, and who your artists are. Use all the descriptive words you can think of. It might even help to make a list of all the things you *aren't*.

This list can guide many of your future decisions, from the big ones about which artists to sign, to the little ones about what color your postcards should be. Who you are drives what you say about yourself to others. Know thyself, and don't waver.

Then, start to develop a notion of how you want your public to see your label. What do you want them to think of you? Before we get too far along in this direction, let me make two crucial points. One, you can control this only so far—so don't panic if you feel misunderstood now and then. More on that later. And two, I'm not advising you to pretend to be something you're not. You need not invent some glamorous self. Effective indie branding is much more about knowing your audience and your artists well and then communicating honestly about them and to them. And you can do that.

We do not have the power to control what people say about us. However, we do have the power to control what we tell people. With this knowledge, we have the ability to guide the perceptions people have both of us and of our companies.

Think of it as being the press secretary for the president of the United States: at some point, the White House's news of the day is released, but the news is spun to work in favor of the president. The press secretary doesn't have the power to alter news events but works to cast the president's involvement in the most positive light possible. In the music business you won't really have too much bad news to announce, not nearly as much as the president does at least, but you will have good news that you want people to know, and from that news people will develop a perception of you as a label. So you always want to give people an accurate picture of what you are trying to accomplish as a company.

The truth always wins. No matter what, the reality about what you are doing as a label and as a collective of music lovers will come through in the end. As a label, you really are only as much as what you do and the music you put out, so you must be able to stand by your work. If you are creepy and are out to exploit the artists you work with and take advantage of them, at some point that truth will be unearthed, and people will resent you. You have chosen to be an active participant in the music business in order to support and further the success of the bands you love. If this is true, people will recognize and appreciate your effort and passion.

Granted, you will always encounter those who gossip and speak negatively about your label. If you don't expect that, I guess I'm breaking some bad news. I can't explain why human nature works this way, but I can testify to you that I've seen it happen, to artists, bands, and labels, over and over again. Maybe people get jealous. Maybe it's being the focus of media attention. Who knows? But part of the gig is that you're going to get talked about, and some of that talk won't be all positive.

I grew up with five older sisters, and from a young age I've been given advice about how to deal with women. The one big lesson my sisters taught me, or at least the one I retained, is: "Now, Ian, girls will either like you or they won't. There is really nothing you can do about that. You can't make a girl do anything and you definitely don't want to go out with a girl who doesn't like you for who you are. So just be yourself, be confident, and if a girl likes you, she'll find a way to make that clear."

This is exactly where we start in the music business. Without mapping out anything, you can get your collective image out there simply by being yourself. You're doing it right now. Just by sitting there, reading this, you are evidently eager to learn more about running a label and probably have a decent work ethic. After all, these books can sometimes be a drag and take a bit of gumption to get through. Kudos.

So do your thing. Focus and work hard. People will like you if they will and they won't if they don't. You can't force the public to like you or like the music you are promoting, but you can provide as many opportunities as possible for people to determine whether or not they do like you and the music you care so much about.

I've talked about how word on the street might surprise you with its occasional negativity. (Don't get discouraged.) But most often, talk can be *very* positive for you! Gossip, conversation, and social networking website exchanges can all help build your image and promote your artists. These conversations all have a point of origin, and sometimes you can create those points and fuel that talk.

First, work hard, do your job well, be honest, and run your business with integrity. That will build your reputation for you, and positive word on the street will do a lot of good work attracting media coverage, good artists, and loyal fans.

Second, do think about intentionally fostering a positive public perception. My favorite story about public perception is Benjamin Franklin's. Being a member of the literary elite and running his own prominent print shop when he was in his twenties meant that he was in the public eye, and he worked hard to project the image of an industrious and tenacious young man (just like an indie-label producer). He relished the perception the public eventually developed of him as hardworking. In his autobiography, Franklin wrote that the "industry visible to our neighbors began to give us character and credit." One of his town's prominent merchants noted that "the industry of that Franklin is superior to anything I ever saw of the kind; I see him still at work when I go home from club, and he is at work again before his neighbors are out of bed."

This is the image you want to project. Franklin did it by burning the lights in his print shop before dawn and after dusk, and by cranking out prodigious amounts of prose. You'll do it with sheer hustle. Answer the phone on the second ring, always return calls, e-mail until your fingers bleed, and sound cheerful and energetic even if you wish you were taking a nap. It's good business, and every conversation with you—and anyone associated with your label—contributes to your image and your brand. You are how you sound and look, on MySpace, Facebook, and Twitter, as well as on album covers and in e-mails.

Make no apologies for being young and inexperienced—you're also authentic and clued in to your generation in a way that no business exec in L.A. can claim. Stay energetic and work harder than anyone else in the industry. It sets you apart from the rest of the pack and wins over the hearts of music lovers everywhere. A good work ethic goes a long way because it represents how passionate you are about the music you are working for. If you are willing to burn the candle at both ends and constantly run the risk of getting ulcers for the music you love, well then, man, that music must be awesome.

You want good things to be associated with your name. You want your brand to conjure joyous thoughts and pleasant emotions, because you want to make people happy with the music you support. Everything that has your name on it, your logo, or the name or photo of a band you work with, must help to further your be-all-and-end-all goal for your image. You are building a brand, and that brand is only as good as you make it.

Branding builds that loyal fan base that keeps coming back for more of, well, you. You want to establish a lasting relationship with your customers. If you do that, then you'll have loyalty and repeat sales. Fans of one of your bands will associate that band with a good label, and may come to embrace a second or third band on your label. Everything you put out will be interesting to them, because you will have never failed them before.

Image

Let's call your new company Thank You for Buying This Book Records (Thankyou Records for short). The image you want to project must be uniform, natural, and, simply put, totally awesome. People must latch on to your image, identify with it, and think of it whenever they hear about a Thankyou Records band. As a small, just-starting-because-you-just-thought-of-it-right-now independent record label, start locally. What are you? You're local. So make the most of that. Tout that when you talk to the media. Brag about your local roots. Tell the story of how you got together at the local coffee shop. Sell your music *to* locals *from* locals.

But this image of community can't be made up. Founding an independent record label—or any business for that matter—on a profound sense of community worth needs to be based on an actual investment in the community. You don't need to provide community service (although it wouldn't hurt), but you do need to pay attention to and help the economic and social growth of local businesses (working with local manufacturers, local artists, and local merchandising companies, and distributing your records to local stores, for instance), other bands (working with and supporting local bands), and the music scene in general (by simply going to shows and being a member of the local music scene).

Your image is also all about the music you'll support. And that will dictate your visual aesthetics. So let's decide. Are you supporting hip-hop? Folk? Alt country? Punk rock? Hardcore? Indie rock? Or pop-punk and emo? I, for one, love indie rock. Anything from Les Savy Fav to the Weakerthans. But hang tight if you're not into the whole indie-rock thing. Whatever you play, whatever kind of music you make, you can follow these examples.

Mission Statement/Goals

Knowing who you are, what do you want to do?

Often, it is helpful to write a mission statement or a statement of purpose outlining your goals and your general vision for the future. Are you about selling music? Breaking into the national scene? Getting small-run albums out there in the local neighborhood? Whatever it is, that's your mission.

Here are a couple good examples of some publicly posted mission statements from three labels.

> Eclectone is a label collective dedicated to supporting the art of songwriting. A cooperative of unique musicians, business people, and writers, we're working to inspire and support both the music and livelihoods of our artists.
>
> Through a cooperative effort, our community-based ideals promote both a way of listening and a way of life. Borne out of love and necessity, Eclectone has become our refuge from the vast machine that has become the modern, corporate-sponsored music business.
>
> Buzz bands, hairstyles, and pop princesses can come and go, but good rock-and-roll songs will never go out of style.
>
> —Eclectone Records

In the first sentence we already get what Eclectone is all about: a supportive collective of songwriters. This sort of language is generally used to describe folk and roots music, which is exactly the kind of music they support. They articulate key terms like *cooperative effort*, *community-based*, and *support*, making it clear that Eclectone focuses on a strong bond between artists within its community and cares a lot about the integrity of the music they release.

> What Goodnight is trying to do—at least, what it thinks it is trying to do (what it tells girls in bars it is doing)—is provide

a conduit for our talented friends to produce, distribute, and promote their work to the rest of the world. Everyone has a brilliant friend. Sometimes we are lucky enough to have two. In our case, well, let's just say we've run out of fingers and toes trying to count up all of our brilliant friends and we are so fortunate to have a little extra cash from our nascent small-arms smuggling enterprise to be able to plow back into recordings of our brilliant amazing friends.

—Goodnight Records

Goodnight Records portrays an image of playful optimism and sneakily gives us the impression that they've really got it where it counts, without sounding like jerks.

So if you feel that community is essential to you, want to start out on the local level, like indie rock, and want to break into the national level, you might start with something like this:

Thankyou Records is an independent, community-based record label that works with young local bands, providing ample support for burgeoning creativity as it moves ever closer to the national stage.

There you go. Now you've got your mission statement for your business plan, your album covers, and your interview with *Spin*.

4

Finding Artists

Everyone I have ever spoken with about what it really takes to find the next big artist has simply said, "Luck." And it is absolutely true. Being at the right place at exactly the right time is the only way to find the right band. But how do you make that happen?

First, it helps to be in the right place. Granted, some towns, cities, and regions have bigger and stronger music scenes than others, but there is always one to find, no matter where you are. If the scene where you are isn't big enough to produce new music and bands, then get in your car. You don't need to live in a big city to start a good indie label, but it doesn't hurt. Bands want to be heard by people, and people who are looking to hear bands go to the city. That's just the way it is. I ran Afternoon Records for four years while going to college in Northfield, Minnesota, a small town an hour south of Minneapolis. The bands weren't in Northfield, they were in Minneapolis and St. Paul, and so I needed to commute. You, too, may have to be willing to make a commute if you're not already living in a music center.

Next, you need to insert yourself into the local music scene and make sure you are hearing the new bands as they emerge and hearing the new music as it is being created. You must find it, get inside it, and make yourself an indispensable and always present part of it. Learn about every band you possibly can, go to a show every night, and learn about the community. And above all, ask yourself the tough questions: Which bands have big draws? Which don't? Which bands do you actually like, and is what you like the same thing that everyone else around you in the music scene likes? Meet people. Meet people who know the people you just met. Meet people and remember their names. You need to make connections and you need to make them fast.

With Afternoon Records, I had the good fortune of being a scene kid since I was fifteen. I went to shows as if I needed music to survive. In the process of simply showing up to concerts, I began to recognize a few of the other regulars and they recognized me. This is a great way to find like-minded people, because if they're going to shows of bands that you like, chances are, you're going to have a lot in common.

When I first started out, I took the approach of working with younger bands who had a youthful and excited following. This meant that most of the artists I worked with were about my age and had fans about our age too. I decided to do this because I thought it made sense for me to grow up with my bands. I knew it would take me a few years to figure out how to run the label. By picking a young group of bands with a young following, I figured that by the time I was old enough to do a good, competitive job of running the label, the bands and their fans would be older, able to go to bars, and well-acquainted with me from the time we were all in high school. In a sense, the label and I grew older and better just as our fan base did—it was a wonderful marriage of good timing and wishful thinking.

Right away, you don't have to go after the big bands that might be considered the obvious choices. In fact, being critically acclaimed is not all it's cracked up to be. Consumer reviews repeatedly predict and dictate sales trends more accurately than do critics. With that in mind, not every release you bring into the world needs to strike a chord with critics, but it does need to strike a chord with buyers.

The moral of the story is that you should work with what you know and what you like, because it is more *you* in the end. Ultimately, that will deliver a more natural feel and sound.

5

Attorneys

Ever since I was a small child, popular culture has taught me that lawyers are not to be trusted. Whether it was an episode of *The Simpsons* in which all humankind held hands around the Earth to celebrate the absence of attorneys, or some Looney Tunes character dropping an anvil on the head of an unfortunate suit-clad man carrying a briefcase, I got the picture: attorneys are evil.

They're really not all that bad. Granted, their services cost an exorbitant amount of money that is difficult for most musicians and label owners to shoulder, but an attorney's services are vital to the success of business deals within the music world. Artists and label owners need to understand each other. Blocks to communication are early hurdles to overcome when beginning a working relationship, and this is where attorneys lend a helping hand.

I have been in the middle of situations where this terrible sentence has been uttered: "Oh, well, that's not what I meant." That is the worst. A spit and a handshake sounds great in theory and even works sometimes, but really, what harm could come from clearly outlining the expectations of both parties? It takes a bit of time and planning now, but it's totally worth it in the end. Among musicians and companies, and between musicians and companies (and even independent contractors), expectations need to be clear as a bell.

For example, let's pretend that Vagrant Records needs a new distribution deal and EMI comes along with an offer. Vagrant cannot simply say "Cool" and proceed. Each side needs to articulate all their terms and stipulations, even if the deal is beyond simple. In that case, an attorney can help simplify the deal.

EMI/Vagrant Distribution Deal

EMI will distribute Vagrant's releases for a commission.

Well, that sounds great, but there are tons of questions lurking in that statement. For instance, what will the commission be? Where will the records be distributed? Does this include digital distribution? How many units will EMI need from Vagrant as a minimum order? Is this an exclusive deal? Will this apply to every Vagrant release, or just a select few that EMI chooses? Does the commission change over time? For example, what happens if a Vagrant release sells more than a million copies? How long will records be in stores? How long will this distribution deal last? And, most important, when will EMI pay Vagrant? And that is just the tip of the iceberg.

Now, let's mock up a contract that addresses these issues. It also assures that both parties will have a greater understanding about what to expect from each other and will therefore be much happier in the end.

EMI will distribute Vagrant's releases for a commission of 30 percent for each unit sold in the territory of the World. EMI will distribute exclusively every release by Vagrant Records to both independent and major brick-and-mortar retailers and all major digital retailers.

EMI will require a minimum of 5,000 units to be shipped to retailers, which will be serviced to retailers for a minimum of six (6) months unless agreed upon otherwise in writing.

EMI will pay Vagrant on a quarterly basis for product sold.

Getting the wording right is one of the main reasons to employ an attorney—to fill in the gaps, apply the correct language to the deal, ask all the right questions, and address all parties' concerns to ensure the clearest outline and greatest understanding.

However, your attorney can do a whole lot more than just serving as a record label owners' babysitter. Finding a good attorney is something you can do now, while you're still reading this book, so that when you do find that great first band, you'll be ready to sign them without delay. In the music business, tasks are specialized. For example, a booking agent only books shows. A distributor only distributes. Managers, although they do a lot, can do that for only a few artists at a time. But an attorney can help you in most if not all aspects of setting up your label, working with your artists, and working with your venues and vendors. Having an attorney makes you look more professional, and it will also help you *be* more professional. A good attorney will ask you all the right questions (and some you might naturally overlook) to help you produce good deals, good contracts, and good relationships. Start asking around and checking out entertainment lawyers near you.

In 2006, my band, One for the Team, headed out on a modest two-week East Coast tour to promote our then new record. While we schlepped our equipment and ourselves across the country as best we could in an oil-belching, broken-down van, I started to receive phone calls from labels interested in working with us. Naturally, I was excited but also completely freaked out. I was nineteen years old and in completely over my head. I was hearing from A&R types representing labels that I had never heard of because they were small or not producing bands I knew, and at the same time from huge labels like Virgin and Epic who, on the other hand, were too intimidating to be taken seriously by me, a guy who didn't think of his band as anything more than a healthy hobby. On top of that, I was hearing from attorneys looking to represent us.

This was new to me. I had never heard of an attorney getting involved on the ground floor with a band, but, as I soon learned, it happens all the time. Here's the angle: if an attorney stumbles upon a hip new band, gets ahold of them first before any labels get wind of the band, and then pitches the band to labels, the attorney earns himself or herself a nice commission—and gets to play a major role in the music world.

A good entertainment attorney always has his or her ear to the ground. With their divining rods attuned to music industry gossip, news, and hearsay, entertainment attorneys generally know which labels are looking for new artists and hopefully what kind of artists those labels are looking for. And if a band fits, it could be a match made in attorney-provided heaven.

Here's the incentive: if an attorney makes a good match, the attorney receives a commission of the recording advance the artist receives, which is generally 10 percent. On top of that, now that this attorney has worked so hard to get the band a record deal, the band would be silly not to retain the same hardworking attorney to negotiate the deal, which would then include the attorney's hourly rate.

This is exactly what happened when One for the Team signed to the Militia Group. I got burned out on A&R people calling at strange hours and talking in those overly suave *I'm-from-one-of-the-coasts-and-you're-from-the-Midwest, that's-so-cute* voices. Instead, I started to listen to the attorneys who were also leaving messages.

One message caught my attention. It was more of a gut instinct really, and that's how I operate. I trust my gut, but I also add some research and track down references. If you feel confident about an attorney who is prospecting you, and it seems like he or she is actually listening to you and cares about what you have to say, then trust the connection (after you do the research and check the references).

What made me choose our attorney from the several who pitched us? First, he was positive. As I said, I was receiving a lot of business calls at that time, and many of the would-be agents and attorneys spent a good part of their conversation engaged in overzealous shit-talking. In some cases they were correct—there are, of course, some bad businesspeople out there, and telling stories is part of the business. But sometimes when people talk such trash, they come off as just trying to make themselves look better—and I don't know about you, but I hate that. Most folks who called me wanted to know who else was calling me, maybe to see if we really were on the buzz radar. When I answered honestly, the party on the other end would often say something like, "Oh no, don't talk to them. They're shady," or, "Yeah, they *used* to be good. But they haven't done anything that good since grunge," blah, blah, blah.

The attorney that won me over got my attention by simply stating, "I bet you're getting a ton of annoying phone calls from industry types. That's a drag." I agreed with him. We started to work together.

Our connection comes in handy in many ways. I use an attorney for contract and business advice and help. I also use an attorney now and then for my personal, strange, and twisted version of A&R, in which an attorney, rather than a label representative, finds the talent.

Now that I've worked with my attorney for some years, he and I know each other pretty well. He gives me band tips, and I give him some too. The postal carrier brings me thousands of submissions, most of which are unsolicited, each year. While I enjoy looking and listening through these when time allows, time often doesn't allow. A tip from an attorney about a new band carries more weight.

Attorneys can help you not only with business dealings but as another pair of in-the-know ears out there, feeding you band names. That's good value.

Now that you know that you cannot go on another day without an attorney, how do you get one? Ask around. Ask other labels. Ask other artists.

Bands and labels are generally forthcoming with a name and a recommendation if asked earnestly. Although it is important to listen to what people have to say about an attorney, be sure also to gather enough information so you can form an opinion for yourself. You never know. A bad story may be the tale of one bad day in the life of an otherwise talented attorney. Dig a little. Also hit handy websites like findlaw.com and dexknows.com that list attorneys by both type and region.

When stepping into the hunt, don't forget the work you've already done developing your mission and image. Try to match an attorney with your label's personality. Don't get an "I like to party and hang out" attorney if you don't like to party and hang out. Be true to who you are when you hire an attorney so that it will be natural for the attorney to honor your nature and your work.

6

Record Deals

Types of Recording Deals

*T*here are three types of deals that most independent labels (including mine) tend to use, with some variations. None has an official title, but for fun and the sake of simplicity, I will call them honor system agreements, joint ventures, and mirror major deals.

I started out running Afternoon Records on what I called honor system agreements. The contracts were overtly simple and the deal was structured like this: the label pays for everything; the label recoups costs fully through all album sales at shows, in stores, and online; after all costs are reimbursed, the band and the label split everything fifty-fifty.

However, I found that this limited the roles of both the artist and the label, and I slowly but surely worked my way into doing joint ventures. I've used two types of joint ventures. The first one is similar to honor system agreements in the sense that the label pays for everything up front, but then the revenue from CDs and T-shirts is put into one big JV (joint venture) pile. From that pile is first subtracted the label's costs (nonrecoupables such as manufacturing and advertising), then the remainder is divided in half and split equally between artist and label. The label then recoups its advance to the artist (whatever the label gives the artists "in advance" in order to record the album) through the artist's 50 percent share.

Another inventive type of joint venture is a fifty-fifty split between the label and the artist of both the investment as well as the costs. When the band has its own money invested in the project, they may have greater reason to work harder to push CD sales, more inclination to tour and play gigs, and a tendency to make a more sustained effort to generate revenue. When I've run this type of deal with artists, both sides have found this an agreeable and comfortable situation, with great results. The debt incurred by the artists really has motivated them to work a bit harder, and they were sure to get "their money's worth" out of my work, because, after all, they had invested their own money in their project.

The final type of deal I call mirror major. It's similar to the infamous "360 deal" that major labels often use, which gives them a piece of all aspects of the band, including its shows, merchandising, and sales. Most major-ish deals are hard on bands and good for labels. Royalties for the first LP are 13 percent or less, and the band has to pay back the label all the recoupable costs—with less than a dollar-per-album income. If the label gives the band an $8,000 advance, the band needs to sell roughly 8,000 albums—and that's just to pay back the label. *Then* the profits start for the band. However, the bigger the label, the better the bargaining chips. If a label has a great history and reputation, and puts publicity and marketing resources behind its releases, that 13 percent can look much more appealing. The point here is that the bigger and better we get as labels, the more negotiating power we have with artists—and the more we can do for them.

Feel free to experiment to find the best fit for you and for your label's mission. If there is one thing for sure about recording contracts, it's that there is no single way to do them. Look around, taste a few selections, and put together an agreement that reflects both you as a person and the spirit of the label.

The Recording Contract

Once you've established who you are and what the hell you're doing, you have to go find yourself some bands. Let's pretend. For several months, you've had a few bands on your radar. This is a good plan; look at bands all the time, and always have a few under consideration. A band you especially like, called the Readers, has just finished recording their first full-length record and want to put it out fast, so your learning curve will be rather steep for your first release. You've decided that you want to sign them. Now, how are you going to get them?

You're so smart that you've already read my chapter on finding an attorney, and you're either well along in that process or have already started working with one. However, before your attorney can finesse the language in the contract you want to offer the Readers, you have to sit down and think through how you want this deal to be structured. Ultimately, the purpose of a recording contract with artists is to spell out your expectations of them and their expectations of you.

There are five essential elements that must be included in the contract.

1. The Term of the Agreement

This dictates exactly how long the agreement will endure and also functions as a good opening clause. Here is an example:

Term. This Agreement shall be in effect for [X number of] record(s) from the date listed above. As a result, Artist, both individually and with others, must release all musical material through Thankyou Records, unless Thankyou Records waives this provision in writing in advance.

You need to decide how long you want to work with the Readers and propose that term in your contract negotiations with them. You want an agreement specifying that whatever the Readers do from now on through X number of releases, they will do with you, unless you agree otherwise.

2. Viable Entity

Along with the Term clause, you could (and should) attach a Viable Entity clause that simply states that the band will stay together as a band for as long as the Term agreement indicates. This protects you from bands breaking up in midcontract. (And just try to get your money back from a band that's already scattered to the winds.) The Viable Entity clause also protects you from the band's hiring a substandard replacement player who compromises the quality of recordings and shows. This kind of language is often used to cover this situation:

Viable Entity. Artist agrees to remain a viable entity throughout the term of the contract. All personnel changes of Artist must be approved by Thankyou Records in writing.

3. Artist Advancements

This spells out how much money Thankyou Records will give the Readers, and when. Remember there are two standard agreements that make sense when it comes to this business:

a. The label pays for everything and then the band and the label split the profits fifty-fifty after the label has recouped its investment.
b. The label and the band invest equal amounts of money into one large pool. The label recoups its investment first, the band recoups its investment second, and then the band and the label split the profits fifty-fifty.

Let's plan on covering all of the artist's expenses and then splitting the proceeds. Here's an example of what that could look like:

<u>Advances/Recording Funds</u>. Artist acknowledges that all costs funded by Thankyou Records on behalf of Artist (which may include, by way of example only, studio, manufacturing, and advertising) are considered part of an Artist Advancement, unless otherwise agreed upon in writing between Artist and Thankyou Records. At the completion of each project, Thankyou Records will recoup all artist advancements through LP sales. So long as Artist is in full compliance with this Agreement, Thankyou Records will not direct reimbursement from Artist for these costs.

4. Royalties

Royalties are payments that you make to the band for each recording sold. A Royalty clause looks like this:

a. Each record sale will be divided as follows in regards to royalties:
  i. *Before* Thankyou Records has recouped Artist Advance in Full:
    100 percent to Artist Advance Recouping (Thankyou Records)
  ii. *After* Thankyou Records has recouped Artist Advance in full:
    50 percent to Thankyou Records
    50 percent to Artist

5. Rerelease of Materials

Once you produce the Readers' first LP, promote their tour, and publicize them all over the region, you want the proceeds of your labor to come to you—not to another label that comes along and snaps up the band. The Rerelease clause protects labels against bands rereleasing material the label has helped produce and promote for a period of time. This clause typically ensures that the master cannot be released for five years following its initial release. Such a clause would look like this:

Rerelease of Material. Artist shall not rerelease any material produced with Thankyou Records for a term of five (5) years from the date of original release of said material, unless Thankyou Records gives its express permission in writing in advance.

These five contract elements are crucial. Contracts can include other clauses and cover other matters, but these five lay the foundation.

Here's an example of a typical contract in full, similar to the contract I developed for Afternoon Records over a month or two of asking questions of our attorney and spending some time in the contractual law section of the library, looking up examples and advice.

ARTIST AGREEMENT

This Agreement is made and entered into this ____ day of _____, _____, by and between Thankyou Records and **the Readers** (hereinafter "Artist"). Artist is composed of the following individuals, all of whom agree to the terms of and are bound by this Agreement as individuals, as well as members of Artist:

(List the band members' names here.)

In consideration of the mutual covenants herein contained and other good and valuable consideration, the parties agree as follows:

1. Territory and Recording Commitment.

    a. Territory. The territory subject to this Agreement shall be the entire World known as planet Earth (the "Territory") and any other planets, for that matter.

    b. Product Commitment.

        i. Within three (3) months following the Effective Date, Artist shall deliver to Thankyou Records one (1) LP (referred to herein as the "first LP").

        ii. Thankyou Records shall have one (1) option (the "Option") to require Artist to deliver one (1) additional LP as defined as a full-length album (referred to herein as the "second LP"). Thankyou Records may exercise the Option by giving written notice to Artist at any time within eighteen (18) months following the delivery of the first LP. Artist shall deliver the second LP, if applicable, no later than thirty-six (36) months after Artist delivered the first LP.

iii. Artist, both individually and with others, must release all musical material through Thankyou Records, unless Thankyou Records waives this provision in writing in advance. However, as noted below, some terms of this Agreement shall survive the release.

2. <u>Grant of Rights</u>.

a. Artist and Thankyou Records will jointly (50 percent Thankyou Records / 50 percent Artist) own the Masters and artwork throughout the Territory, and all Masters delivered hereunder will be regarded as works for hire under United States copyright law, and such Masters shall be registered jointly in the names of Artist and Thankyou Records. If the Masters are not considered to be works for hire under United States copyright law, then Artist agrees to transfer in perpetuity its interest to Thankyou Records so that Artist and Thankyou Records jointly own the Masters and artwork.

b. Artist warrants, represents, and agrees that throughout the Territory, Thankyou Records shall have the exclusive right by any media now known or hereafter devised to use, control, manufacture, sell, distribute (including remote delivery and/or electronic distribution), promote, advertise, lease, synch with any medium, license, or otherwise exploit commercially, promotionally, or otherwise all Masters delivered hereunder and all artwork created during the term for use in connection therewith. Thankyou Records shall have the right to adapt the Masters to conform to emerging technological formats; provided, however, Thankyou Records shall not have the right to alter the Masters for any purpose other than technical conformity with such emerging formats without Artist's express written consent (for example, Thankyou Records shall not have the right to remix or edit the Masters without Artist's express written consent).

c. Thankyou Records and its designees shall have the nonexclusive right to use the name and likeness of Artist, the individual producer, and all other persons performing services in connection with Masters (including, without limitation, all professional, group, and other assumed or fictitious names used by them), and biographical material concerning Artist and them for purposes of advertising, promotion, and trade in connection with the exploitation of the Masters and records and videos hereunder and the general goodwill advertising of Thankyou Records. Artist shall be available from time to time as reasonably directed by Thankyou Records to appear for photography and other artwork, and for interviews.

3. Advances/Recording Funds.

a. Artist acknowledges that all costs funded by Thankyou Records on behalf of Artist (which may include, by way of example only, studio, manufacturing, and advertising) are considered part of an Artist Advancement, unless otherwise agreed upon in writing between Artist and Thankyou Records. At the completion of each project, Thankyou Records will recoup all Artist Advancements through LP sales, licensing, and merchandise sales.

b. Tour support and Recording Advance with respect to the first LP, which shall be regarded as a Royalty Advance as defined herein, shall be Ten Thousand Dollars and No/100 ($10,000.00).

c. Any additional payments by Thankyou Records to Artist for any reason whatsoever shall be regarded as Advances, as defined herein.

4. Royalties.

a. Each record sale will be divided as follows in regards to royalties:

i. *Before* Thankyou Records has recouped Artist Advance in Full:
100 percent to Artist Advance Recouping (Thankyou Records)

ii. *After* Thankyou Records has recouped Artist Advance in full:

50 percent to Thankyou Records

50 percent to Artist

b. In addition to paying all Costs hereunder, Thankyou Records may, from time to time, advance money and/or merchandise to Artist for any reason whatsoever, which shall be considered tour support. Such advance payments (the "Advances") shall be recoupable by Thankyou Records from royalties otherwise payable to Artist following recoupment of all Costs as defined herein. Advances by Thankyou Records to Artist hereunder shall be made at Thankyou Records' sole discretion.

5. <u>Licensing of Masters</u>. Thankyou Records shall notify Artist of any proposed license (each a "Licensing Event") with respect to the Masters hereunder for synchronization with any motion picture, television, advertising use, etc. Artist shall have the right to reasonably object to any proposed Licensing Event. Thankyou Records shall not grant any license over Artist's reasonable objection, nor shall Thankyou Records refuse to grant any license against Artist's reasonable wishes. Income from said Licensing Event shall be split fifty-fifty (in terms of 50 percent to Artist and 50 percent to Thankyou Records); however, if there is still an outstanding recoupable, all monies incurred by Thankyou Records shall be attributed to the remaining recoupable.

6. <u>Viable Entity</u>. Artist agrees to remain a viable entity throughout the term of the contract. All personnel changes of Artist must be approved by Thankyou Records in writing. In terms of viable entity, Artist will remain available for promoting the album (press, radio, television) for the duration of the release within reason and in good faith.

7. <u>Rerelease of Material</u>. Artist shall not rerelease any material produced with Thankyou Records for a term of five (5) years from the date of original release of said material, unless Thankyou Records gives its express permission in writing in advance.

8. <u>Satisfaction of Delivery</u>. Artist agrees to a satisfaction of delivery commitment. Artist must promote itself in the style and genre that it has been signed under.

9. Artwork. Thankyou Records retains final control of all artwork related to Artist's releases.

10. Performances. Thankyou Records will collect a 10 percent booking commission for all moneys paid out to artists at Thankyou Records–booked shows. In the case of shows sponsored by Thankyou Records, Thankyou Records will determine, at its sole discretion, the amount of Artist payment (this pertains exclusively to the album's release show[s] and label showcases). Artist may play any other show booked by any other party. This commission pertains only to shows booked by Thankyou Records.

11. Renewal. This contract may be renewed or amended at any time by written agreement between Artist and Thankyou Records.

12. Survival of Terms. Clauses 3, 4, 5, 6, and 8 will remain in full force and effect after the term of the Agreement has expired.

13. Ability to Perform. Artist certifies that it may enter into this Agreement and perform all of its terms, and that the terms of this Agreement do not conflict with any other agreements of Artist. Artist agrees to hold Thankyou Records harmless and indemnify Thankyou Records for any damages, including, but not limited to, attorneys' fees and costs, incurred by Thankyou Records in connection with any dispute over the ability of Artist to enter into this Agreement without violating the terms of another agreement.

14. Liability. In addition to any other damages suffered by Thankyou Records, any breach by Artist of any terms of this Agreement will result in Artist's liability to Thankyou Records for all Artist Advancements unrecouped at the time of said breach. In the event of a breach of any term by Artist, Artist agrees to pay Thankyou Records, in addition to any and all other remedies available to Thankyou Records in law and/or equity, all costs and attorneys' fees incurred by Thankyou Records in connection with said breach.

15. Modifications in Writing. These terms and conditions constitute the entire agreement between Artist and Thankyou Records, and may not be modified, changed, or terminated in any way except by written agreement between Artist and Thankyou Records.

16. Venue/Choice of Laws. Any legal action pertaining to this Agreement shall be resolved under the laws of the State of _____, and shall be venued in _____ County, _____.

17. Right to Consult Attorney. All parties acknowledge that this is a legally binding contract; they have reviewed and understand its contents, and have had the opportunity to consult with an attorney of their choice.

IN WITNESS WHEREOF, the parties hereto have read and executed this Agreement the day and year first above stated.

THANKYOU RECORDS

By: (Your name), Co-Owner

ARTIST: *The Readers*

By: (The band members sign here.)

By: _____

By: _____

By: _____

The Annotated Contract

Okay, now let's break this down and start talking about specifics.

1. Territory and Recording Commitment.
   a. Territory. The territory subject to this Agreement shall be the entire World known as planet Earth (the "Territory") and any other planets, for that matter.

The Territory commitment maps out the territory in which your agreement will be valid. It articulates the region or regions in which this release will apply. So we have "the entire world" listed as the region for this release, which may not be the case for every release. For instance, you could have only the rights to release the record in North America because another label owns the rights to release it in Britain, or Europe, or some other region.

b. <u>Product Commitment</u>.
   i. Within three (3) months following the Effective Date, Artist shall deliver to Thankyou Records one (1) LP (referred to herein as the "first LP").

This clause indicates that the artist must finish and have their record ready to be released within the time period of three months after signing. It also spells out what the record must be—the equivalent of an LP or full-length record. Alter these facts to suit each individual situation. For example, if you're releasing EPs because the band has only two songs, try this:

   i. Within three (3) months following the Effective Date, Artist shall deliver to Thankyou Records one (1) EP (referred to herein as the "first EP").
   ii. Thankyou Records shall have one (1) option (the "Option") to require Artist to deliver one (1) additional EP as defined as an extended play (referred to herein as the "second EP"). Thankyou Records may exercise the Option by giving written notice to Artist at any time within eighteen (18) months following the delivery of the first EP. Artist shall deliver the second EP, if applicable, no later than thirty-six (36) months after Artist delivered the first EP.

This clause plans a little bit for the future. The first important aspect of it is the "option." The option is an interesting concept because it gives the label the right of first refusal. The band is obligated to release its next record with Thankyou Records, but Thankyou Records is not obligated to release the band's next anything. In short, Thankyou Records has first dibs on the next record, but has the "option" to say no and pass on the release—even though the band does not have the same luxury.

What would drive you to exercise the option? If the release flops mega-ultra-big-time, or the band is not working very hard (not touring, not returning phone calls, etc.) or has developed a bad attitude, you may feel grateful to have the option of taking a pass on their next release.

On the other hand, let's flip the situation on its head. Let's say that the band is extraordinarily unhappy working with you. It's just not working out, and there isn't much you can do about it. In that case, wouldn't you rather work with a band that is happy to call you home? I know I would. So if a band is no longer into your label, maybe that's another good sign that it's time to let them go.

The benefit of the option does not apply only to the release of an artist into the abyss of label-less-ness, but also to the situation of releasing them to another label. Much of what an indie label does is prep a band for future success. If you're doing your job, you're locating fledgling talent and developing it. Bigger labels are bound to come along to take a look at one, many, or all of your artists at some point. Why wouldn't they? You have amazing taste.

With that in mind, this option gives you a bargaining chip—a big bargaining chip. Let's say that you've signed the Readers, put out an LP, and Barsuk Records comes knocking on your door and is simply in love with the Readers. Barsuk wants to pick them up as soon as possible and upstream (rerelease and distribute widely) all of their past releases. Now you can talk, and now you might make yourself a little money. This option has made certain that you own the next record the Readers put out. This gives you a lot of control.

With this option, Barsuk needs to negotiate with you. Barsuk might pay you to buy that option away from you, or might work with you in any one of a number of creative ways. You've invested in this band, and this is part of how you make your money for the services you render. This option puts you at the table in these discussions in the position of a negotiator—if not the prime negotiator. You'll get something for your efforts, and you can also help the band get the best deal possible.

iii. Artist, both individually and with others, must release all musical material through Thankyou Records, unless Thankyou Records waives this provision in writing in advance. However, as noted below, some terms of this Agreement shall survive the release.

Now that the band has signed with you, the Readers must run everything musical that they do past you first. If the bass player has an indie-pop-dance side project that she wants to pursue, she needs to let you know what she is up to and her plans for the project. If she is the principal songwriter, and you like her stuff, then you may want first dibs to release her new project. Chances are, if she is a member of a band that you think is great, her side project might also be pretty awesome. Granted, if she is not a principal member of the other band, it may not be worth the trouble of connecting these dots, so you have the option of "waiving" this clause, meaning you do not want to be involved with the project.

2. Grant of Rights.

a. Artist and Thankyou Records will jointly (50 percent Thankyou Records / 50 percent Artist) own the Masters and artwork throughout the Territory, and all Masters delivered hereunder will be regarded as works for hire under United States copyright law, and such Masters shall be registered jointly in the names of Artist and Thankyou Records. If the Masters are not considered to be works for hire under United States copyright law, then Artist agrees to transfer in perpetuity its interest to Thankyou Records so that Artist and Thankyou Records jointly own the Masters and artwork.

Under the first clause under Grant of Rights, you spell out that the artist and the label will jointly own the masters and artwork of this release. Most labels own 100 percent of the master disc, which is something that you can do, but for now, I like to think about matters like this in a bit more of an egalitarian sense. This becomes important down the road when ownership becomes a big deal. Let's dip back into the Barsuk deal. If they would like to rerelease all of the Readers' back catalog, then they need to acquire the masters. In this case, they would have to buy 50 percent from the artist and 50 percent from us—yet another bargaining chip worth having.

> b. Artist warrants, represents, and agrees that throughout the Territory, Thankyou Records shall have the exclusive right by any media now known or hereafter devised to use, control, manufacture, sell, distribute (including remote delivery and/or electronic distribution), promote, advertise, lease, synch with any medium, license, or otherwise exploit commercially, promotionally, or otherwise all Masters delivered hereunder and all artwork created during the term for use in connection therewith. Thankyou Records shall have the right to adapt the Masters to conform to emerging technological formats; provided, however, that Thankyou Records shall not have the right to alter the Masters for any purpose other than technical conformity with such emerging formats without Artist's express written consent (for example, Thankyou Records shall not have the right to remix or edit the Masters without Artist's express written consent).

This clause solidifies the fact that yes, indeed, Thankyou Records is the artist's label and has the exclusive right to control all of the artist's affairs. In other words, Thankyou Records, and only Thankyou Records, is the label to call when anyone in the world wants to talk about the artist.

Beyond that, since technology is always changing and who the heck really knows what will come after the household use of MP3s, this clause also stipulates that Thankyou Records has the rights to this music in any past, present, or future medium by which music will be transmitted. This protects you in the sense that if Apple Computer comes up with an audio chip that can be put in someone's brain or if they find a way to give someone the ability to download a song directly into their cerebral cortex simply by thinking about it, then we still own the rights to those brainwave-transmitted songs.

This restricts your rights a bit too. You do not have the right to change the masters in any way unless you need to adapt to future technology. So you can't remix the tracks or the whole album without the written consent of the artist. It doesn't matter how good you are with Reason and Pro Tools, you just don't have the right.

> c. Thankyou Records and its designees shall have the nonexclusive right to use the name and likeness of Artist, the individual producer, and all other persons performing services in connection with Masters (including, without limitation, all professional, group, and other assumed or fictitious names used by them), and biographical material concerning Artist and them for purposes of advertising, promotion, and trade in connection with the exploitation of the Masters and records and videos hereunder and the general goodwill advertising of Thankyou Records. Artist shall be available from time to time as reasonably directed by Thankyou Records to appear for photography and other artwork, and for interviews.

This clause indicates that Thankyou Records will use promotional photos, one-sheets, press releases, artwork, etc. to promote and get the word out about the band and, in turn, the band must make itself available to help out a bit. You don't want to work hard to get interviews and photo shoots and then find yourself with a band that won't agree to show up and be interviewed and photographed.

3. Advances/Recording Funds.
> a. Artist acknowledges that all costs funded by Thankyou Records on behalf of Artist (which may include, by way of example only, studio, manufacturing, and advertising) are considered part of an Artist Advancement, unless otherwise agreed upon in writing be-

tween Artist and Thankyou Records. At the completion of each project, Thankyou Records will recoup all Artist Advancements through LP sales, licensing, and merchandise sales.

This clause spells out exactly what the advance is. Labels do this differently. Some consider the advance to be strictly a recording budget, others consider it a cash handout to help persuade the artist to sign with them. I tend to look at it as the overall budget: this is all the money that will be used for promoting, marketing, and recording your artist. How this advance is spent, or allocated, should be decided between the artist and the label—you want some control and you want to work together to spend the money in a way that both the band and the label find wise and productive.

b. Tour support and Recording Advance with respect to the first LP, which shall be regarded as a Royalty Advance as defined herein, shall be Ten Thousand Dollars and No/100 ($10,000.00).

This clause states the amount of money that you agree to put into the advance. In this case it is $10,000. Every budget is different for every release, so this number changes contract to contract. This clause may be the most important element of the contract to most or all of the people involved in this deal. This will likely be the ultimate "now we are all on the same page" clause.

c. Any additional payments by Thankyou Records to Artist for any reason whatsoever shall be regarded as Advances, as defined herein.

This is the "just in case" clause that covers emergencies. Say the Readers get in the middle of Nowhere, North Dakota, and don't have enough money for food or gas. You wire them a few hundred bucks, but you call that an "advance" and it falls under all the terms you've stipulated here about how you're going to handle advances.

<u>Royalties</u>.

    a. Each record sale will be divided as follows in regards to royalties:

        i. *Before* Thankyou Records has recouped Artist Advance in Full: 100 percent to Artist Advance Recouping (Thankyou Records)

        ii. *After* Thankyou Records has recouped Artist Advance in full:

        50 percent to Thankyou Records

        50 percent to Artist

Depending on the kind of deal you are working, you can divide royalties in a variety of ways. In general, I've worked deals in such a way that the label covers all the expenses, then recoups those expenses first through album sales, licensing, and merchandise, and then, after having fully recouped, the artist and the label split the proceeds equally. This is a really easy and clear way to handle things, and I have just found it most beneficial to keep things simple. However, there are other types of deals, and I'll outline those later.

    b. In addition to paying all Costs hereunder, Thankyou Records may, from time to time, advance money and/or merchandise to Artist for any reason whatsoever, which shall be considered tour support. Such advance payments (the "Advances") shall be recoupable by Thankyou Records from royalties otherwise payable to Artist following recoupment of all Costs as defined herein. Advances by Thankyou Records to Artist hereunder shall be made at Thankyou Records' sole discretion.

This clause creates the safeguard that Thankyou Records will be able to contribute to the original advance at any later date, if and when the artist needs greater support, and that that contribution will be added to the amount agreed upon as the advance.

5. <u>Licensing of Masters</u>. Thankyou Records shall notify Artist of any proposed license (each a "Licensing Event") with respect to the Masters hereunder for synchronization with any motion picture, television,

advertising use, etc. Artist shall have the right to reasonably object to any proposed Licensing Event. Thankyou Records shall not grant any license over Artist's reasonable objection, nor shall Thankyou Records refuse to grant any license against Artist's reasonable wishes. Income from said Licensing Event shall be split fifty-fifty (in terms of 50 percent to Artist and 50 percent to Thankyou Records); however, if there is still an outstanding recoupable, all monies incurred by Thankyou Records shall be attributed to the remaining recoupable.

If a prospective licensor would like to place a song in a movie, commercial, or television show, Thankyou Records must consult with the artist about what exactly the placement will be and where it will occur. If Outback Steakhouse would like to place in a nation-wide commercial a song written by a band composed of vegans, the band just might take issue with the placement. So it's always best to make sure you get the a-okay from all parties involved. If everybody is cool with the placement, then the artist and Thankyou Records would split the income in half. I'll talk more about licensing in a later chapter.

6. <u>Viable Entity</u>. Artist agrees to remain a viable entity throughout the term of the contract. All personnel changes of Artist must be approved by Thankyou Records in writing. In terms of viable entity, Artist will remain available for promoting the album (press, radio, television) for the duration of the release within reason and in good faith.

This clause simply states that Thankyou Records would really like it if the artist continued to produce music, and so, in the event that the artist stops performing or the band breaks up, this would be considered a breach of contract.

7. <u>Rerelease of Material</u>. Artist shall not rerelease any material produced with Thankyou Records for a term of five (5) years from the date of original release of said material, unless Thankyou Records gives its express permission in writing in advance.

This clause states that the artist cannot rerelease any material that was released on Thankyou Records elsewhere within five years after signing. An artist who released a record on Thankyou Records will not be able to put any of those same songs on another label's record without permission from Thankyou Records.

8. <u>Satisfaction of Delivery</u>. Artist agrees to a satisfaction of delivery commitment. Artist must promote itself in the style and genre that it has been signed under.

This clause ensures that when Thankyou Records signs an artist, the artist will write and perform the music for which they were signed. For instance, if you sign a hip-hop artist, they should make hip-hop music and not, suddenly, metal.

9. <u>Artwork</u>. Thankyou Records retains final control of all artwork related to Artist's releases.

Just in case the artist provides album artwork that is horribly offensive or simply bad, Thankyou Records is able to pull the plug and ask for a redesign.

10. <u>Performances</u>. Thankyou Records will collect a 10 percent booking commission for all moneys paid out to artists at Thankyou Records–booked shows. In the case of shows sponsored by Thankyou Records, Thankyou Records will determine, at its sole discretion, the amount of Artist payment (this pertains exclusively to the album's release show[s] and label showcases). Artist may play any other show booked by any other party. This commission pertains only to shows booked by Thankyou Records.

This stipulates that if Thankyou Records books a show for an artist, it will receive 10 percent of what the artist gets paid. But the artist can book and play any other show without owing a commission to Thankyou Records.

11. <u>Renewal</u>. This contract may be renewed or amended at any time by written agreement between Artist and Thankyou Records.

This clause creates a degree of flexibility within the contract such that if any agreeing party has an issue with it after signing, they are allowed to talk about it. For instance, if Thankyou Records adds a full-blown booking division, the language and concepts behind booking performances would likely change. Or, if the royalty or tour support policy should change for any future releases, the contract can be revised. New ideas are the lifeblood of an ever evolving industry; therefore, your contracts should be ever evolving as well.

12. <u>Survival of Terms</u>. Clauses 3, 4, 5, 6, and 8 will remain in full force and effect after the term of the Agreement has expired.

The survival of a few clauses in this contract is important, because, even if the band stops making music, it is Thankyou Records' duty to fulfill some obligations: paying royalties, maintaining licensing rights, etc.

13. <u>Ability to Perform</u>. Artist certifies that it may enter into this Agreement and perform all of its terms, and that the terms of this Agreement do not conflict with any other agreements of Artist. Artist agrees to hold Thankyou Records harmless and indemnify Thankyou Records for any damages, including, but not limited to, attorneys' fees and costs, incurred by Thankyou Records in connection with any dispute over the ability of Artist to enter into this Agreement without violating the terms of another agreement.

This clause ensures that the artist and Thankyou Records both have the legal authority to enter into this contract and plan to fulfill the terms to each party's best ability. Which, in other words, means that the artist should not have a super-secret contract with another label.

14. <u>Liability</u>. In addition to any other damages suffered by Thankyou Records, any breach by Artist of any terms of this Agreement will result in Artist's liability to Thankyou Records for all Artist Advancements unrecouped at the time of said breach. In the event of a breach of any term by Artist, Artist agrees to pay Thankyou Records, in addition to any and all other remedies available to Thankyou Records in law and/or equity, all costs and attorneys' fees incurred by Thankyou Records in connection with said breach.

If the contract is breached by the artist, then the artist owes the advance back to Thankyou Records. This generally happens only in response to extreme events—for the most part, breaches of contract can be sorted out between the parties before this point is reached.

15. <u>Modifications in Writing</u>. These terms and conditions constitute the entire agreement between Artist and Thankyou Records, and may not be modified, changed, or terminated in any way except by written agreement between Artist and Thankyou Records.

In the event that one party would like to make a change, it must be brought up with the other, discussed, and agreed upon in writing.

16. <u>Venue/Choice of Laws</u>. Any legal action pertaining to this Agreement shall be resolved under the laws of the State of _____, and shall be venued in _____ County, _____.

If there is a legal dispute, this clause indicates that it must be sorted out in a court of law within the state of _____. Generally, it's best to have this clause reflect where the label is founded. This is especially important when signing an international artist, whose home country might have different contract laws and traditions.

17. <u>Right to Consult Attorney</u>. All parties acknowledge that this is a legally binding contract; they have reviewed and understand its con-

tents, and have had the opportunity to consult with an attorney of their choice.

This final clause acknowledges that both parties understand that they have the right to consult an attorney in regard to this contract, and that both parties should fully understand the agreement and the implications associated with it before signing. So if they don't consult an attorney, and they find issue with the contract later, they can't complain; they were warned here, after all.

With these tools, you will be sufficiently prepared to see eye-to-eye with your bands. Remember that communication is the most important aspect of—and bad communication the biggest obstacle to—your recording contract. Simpler is better, so keep things clear and succinct, and be sure to run every contract by your attorney before you put it into effect.

7

Copyright

Copyright is all at once the most important, least important, most confusing, and most straightforward element of putting out a record. It's worth your while to do the little bit of homework necessary to truly understand it, however, because copyright provides the foundation on which songwriting and music publishing are based, and it constitutes the most important protection you have both for you and for the products you develop as a label.

Many of the core concepts of copyright have existed since the eighteenth century, which means that it is a ridiculous challenge to make these laws relevant and applicable to current musical media. Much of the language and elements of copyright law have not changed, or have not changed much, since their conception.

A copyright functions as a "limited duration monopoly." It gives the creator of an intellectual property—in this case, a piece of music—exclusive ownership rights to his or her musical work for a finite amount of time.

How do you get a copyright? According to U.S. copyright law, the moment you create something tangible, you possess a copyright. With music, if someone has written a killer song, or even just a killer riff, all that needs to be done to copyright it is either to write it down in musical notation, record it on a tape recorder, record it as an MP3 or even record it onto an answering machine. As long as there is physical evidence to prove that a musical idea exists, then it is owned and so is the copyright.

You might have heard that to ensure a copyright, you should record your work, put it on CD or vinyl or whatever, and then mail it to yourself. You can, but mailing it isn't necessary. But if one of your artists has written a song and has yet to record it, it is not copyrighted. You must make sure that the hits your bands write get onto disc.

Copyrights as I have outlined them above are your band's rights. What are yours as a label? The band has the sole right to perform their songs live at shows, reproduce their work in any format, and distribute that reproduction. As their label, armed with the contract we examined in the previous chapter, you now have the sole right to manufacture CDs and vinyl, release MP3s, and distribute these formats in stores nationwide and to online digital download retailers.

Publishing

An artist–publisher deal is relatively simple at heart. The band writes the songs and *assigns* the copyrights to them to its label. The label seeks buyers to use those songs (buyers such as Apple for iPod commercials or *Grey's Anatomy* for brief segments between shots), negotiates licensing deals with those buyers, ensures that those buyers pay for what they are using, and then splits the proceeds with the artist.

Let me give you an example. One for the Team wrote a great song called "I Promised I'd Grow Up," and released it on Afternoon Records in 2006. In my opinion, that song was just perfect for a Volkswagen commercial. So when One for the Team signed with Afternoon Records, the label then owned the copyright to "I Promised I'd Grow Up" (as well as the rest of the One for the Team catalog, of course). As One for the Team's new publisher, I could send "I Promised I'd Grow Up" to commercial-placement agencies, TV networks, movie studios, etc., asking whether or not they thought the song was suitable for their purposes too. Since I thought the song had especially good possibilities for a Volkswagen commercial, Volkswagen's commercial department was on my list of contacts to send a demo to as well. Let's suppose that after following up diligently (as you must, always), I get Volkswagen to agree (this hasn't actually happened yet . . .): they want to use the song in a commercial promoting the new Jetta series. Volkswagen would then send Afternoon Records, the label/publisher, a ton of paperwork, which we would go through with our attorney and a fine-tooth comb to make sure that both the label and the band understand and agree to every term of the proposed contract. After the contract work and negotiations, let's say Volkswagen offers to pay $10,000 for the use of the song. We say yeah—duh!—and Volkswagen pays either us or One for the Team. Then we split the income.

How exactly we split the $10,000 depends on our particular original licensing deal terms. However, it's a general industry standard that the publisher splits all income with the *writer(s)*, fifty-fifty. Since Afternoon Records already works with fifty-fifty splits for most everything we do, we stick to that because we're familiar with that kind of deal.

Understanding copyright is most likely to be important when you have to deal with licensing on this level; down the road, there may be further implications for some of the music under your label's copyright control.

8

Mechanical Rights

*L*et's backtrack for a moment and review the basics of copyright. The owner of a copyright possesses the exclusive right to reproduce and distribute the musical work they own on so-called phono-records (which is a term that means anything from MP3s, to compact discs, to tapes, to vinyl records, and so on).

Let's break that down a little further. The owner of a copyright possesses the exclusive right to reproduce (manufacture by any means) and distribute (in any manner ranging from in stores, on-line, or handed out to family) the musical work or composition that they own on phonorecords. The owner, and only the owner, has the legal right to take his or her music and create something tangible from it.

The key element of this definition is in the actual creation of a physical or digital musical work. Copyright is created the moment that intellectual property is converted into a tangible physical object such as a CD or vinyl record or a digital file like an MP3. When you take that melody you are hearing in your head, sing it, record it, create a digital file or tape with that recording, and put it out into the world, you establish a right of ownership. The right that I am talking about is known legally as the *mechanical right* or *mechanical license.*

Let's dig a little deeper into the history of mechanical rights to get a better grasp of the issues involved. The U.S. copyright owner's exclusive and solitary ownership of a recording was first addressed by Congress in the Copyright Act of 1909. This act is rather extensive and has been revised many times, most notably in 1976, but here is Section 1 from the original 1909 act, which contains many key passages:

AN ACT TO AMEND AND CONSOLIDATE THE ACTS
RESPECTING COPYRIGHT.
Be it enacted by the Senate and House of Representatives of the United States of America in Congress assembled, That any person entitled thereto, upon complying with the provisions of this Act, shall have the exclusive right:

(a) To print, reprint, publish, copy, and vend the copyrighted work;

(b) To translate the copyrighted work into other languages or dialects, or make any other version thereof, if it be a literary work; to dramatize it if it be a nondramatic work; to convert it into a novel or other nondramatic work if it be a drama; to arrange or adapt it if it be a musical work; to complete, execute, and finish it if it be a model or design for a work of art;

(c) To deliver or authorize the delivery of the copyrighted work in public for profit if it be a lecture, sermon, address, or similar production;

(d) To perform or represent the copyrighted work publicly if it be a drama or, if it be a dramatic work and not reproduced in copies for sale, to vend any manuscript or any record whatsoever thereof; to make or to procure the making of any transcription or record thereof by or from which, in whole or in part, it may in any manner or by any method be exhibited, performed, represented, produced, or reproduced; and to exhibit, perform, represent, produce, or reproduce it in any manner or by any method whatsoever;

(e) To perform the copyrighted work publicly for profit if it be a musical composition and for the purpose of public performance for profit; and for the purposes set forth in subsection (a) hereof, to make any arrangement or setting of it or of the melody of it in any system of notation or any form of record in which the thought of an author may be recorded and from which it may be read or reproduced: *Provided*, That the provisions of this Act, so far as they secure copyright controlling the parts of instruments serving to reproduce mechanically the musical work, shall include only compositions published and copyrighted after this Act goes into effect, and shall not include the works of a foreign author or composer unless the foreign state or nation of which such author or composer is a citizen or subject grants, either by treaty, convention, agreement, or law, to citizens of the United States similar rights: *And provided further, and as a condition of extending the copyright control to such mechanical reproductions*, That whenever the owner of a musical copyright has used or permitted or knowingly acquiesced in the use of the copyrighted work upon the parts of instruments serving to reproduce mechanically the musical work, any other person may make similar use of the copyrighted work upon the payment to the copyright proprietor of a royalty of two cents on each such part manufactured, to be paid by the manufacturer thereof; and the copyright proprietor may require, and if so the manufacturer shall furnish, a report under oath on the twentieth day of each month on the number of parts of instruments manufactured during the previous month serving to reproduce mechanically said musical work, and royalties shall be due on the parts manufactured during any month upon the twentieth of the next succeeding month. The payment of the royalty provided for by this section shall free the articles or devices for which such royalty has been paid from further contribution to the copyright except in case of public performance for profit: *And provided further*, That it shall be the duty of the copyright owner, if he uses the musical composition himself for the manufacture of parts of instruments serving to reproduce mechanically the musical work, or licenses others to do so, to file notice thereof, accompanied by a recording fee, in the copyright office, and any failure to file such notice shall be a complete defense to any suit, action, or proceeding for any infringement of such copyright.

In case of the failure of such manufacturer to pay to the copyright proprietor within thirty days after demand in writing the full sum of royalties due at said rate at the date of such demand the court may award taxable costs to the plaintiff and a reasonable counsel fee, and the court may, in its discretion, enter judgment therein for any sum in addition over the amount found to be due as royalty in accordance with the terms of this Act, not exceeding three times such amount.

The reproduction or rendition of a musical composition by or upon coin-operated machines shall not be deemed a public performance for profit unless a fee is charged for admission to the place where such reproduction or rendition occurs.

In short, this act ensured the owner's right to use and profit from his or her musical work even if they did not own the publishing rights. This act ensures that the writer will always own a mechanical right, which provides for a sometimes lucrative aspect of copyright.

Congress enacted this law to protect composers' mechanical rights, but also to counter the growing threat of musical monopolies at the time. Although it may sound strange to us now, in the early 1900s there was a very real threat of musical monopoly (Apple's iTunes and the iPod often raise the specter of monopoly again, it seems to me). This goes all the way back to the predecessor of the vinyl record: the piano roll. The piano roll was a roll of paper punched with holes. You'd buy a piano roll for a particular song you liked. Then, on a player piano, you'd insert the piano roll onto a metal roller that read the punches and translated them into music by pressing the keys on the piano keyboard. The piano then played itself, and you could hear your favorite song any time you wanted. Piano rolls were manufactured by a pianist sitting down at a special piano that could cut the piano roll as he or she played the tune. The piano roll is considered the first storage medium, a term that now describes anything that can hold music. Today, this term is broadly applied to describe both physical and digital manifestations.

If I may nerd out here for a minute, in the early 1900s, so the story goes, the Aeolian Company dominated piano roll manufacturing and negotiated exclusive production contracts with nearly all the major music publishers of the era. Imagine if there were only one compact disc manufacturing company for all the labels, publishing companies, and artists in the music industry today! Obviously, something needed to change, and section 1 (e) of the 1909 copyright act took care of that.

Section 1 (e) ensured that if the copyright owner used or permitted the use of his or her copyrighted work for reproduction, the owner was entitled to a royalty, called the statutory rate. This statutory rate is a required payment for each song on a record or composed work. In 2009, this rate is 9.1 cents for up to five minutes, and 1.75 cents for every minute after five minutes.

So how does this apply to Thankyou Records? Well, for every retail-ready record you produce for your artists, depending on your contract with each one, the owner of the mechanical right (most likely the songwriter) is entitled to 100 percent of the statutory rate.

Let's kid-size an example of this. Let's say I have a really great recipe for lemonade. I give you the recipe and the right to distribute actual glasses of lemonade, but I would like to maintain my mechanical right, which in this case is the ownership of the recipe I created. Therefore, every time you pour a glass of lemonade and hand it to an eager, thirsty customer, you owe me a royalty because you used my special lemonade recipe.

Back to music. With every unit you sell, you owe your artist $.091 per song on the record. If there are ten songs on an album of which you sell ten copies, you owe the copyright owner $9.10 ($.091 x 10 tracks = $.91, x 10 album sales = $9.10).

This is both what you own and what you owe. If you release a record for an artist, you owe them their royalties, and you own the copyright of the music you produce.

9

How to Approach People and Not Feel Slimy

Now you have your label name. You have defined your label's mission. You have your label's attorney, and you've immersed yourself in your local music scene.

Now that you're a label big enough to be able to approach artists outside your inner circle and your immediate social group, how do you say hello?

I know lots of talented music industry folks who stumble over this same little bit of social awkwardness. When you're working a room for business reasons, it's natural to feel a bit, well, slimy. You're there to make a profit; everyone else in the room is there to hear tunes and meet singles. So how can you break the ice with a band without sounding like a certain protagonist in *Death of a Salesman*?

This is further complicated by the fact that, in the music industry, there *is* something rather, well, slimy about many of the people involved. The industry does attract the fast-buck, fast-talking crowd who can't always deliver what they promise. Just because you're in the industry, and the industry has a certain reputation, through no fault of your own you inherit that bad reputation once you step into the field.

Honestly, the only way to bypass this unfortunate preconception is to be not slimy at all and to just be your honest self. You'll be polite, well-mannered, kind, and clear, and in this way you can both change this image for the better and build a personal reputation for being easy to do business with.

Let's take a moment to think about what makes some industry types slimy. We've all met them. They wear sunglasses indoors and maybe even have a ponytail, and they might have an I-love-hearing-myself-talk-and-I'm-so-great attitude. The way I think of it, if you truly are a great label owner, the band you're talking to already knows that and you need not remind them of it. And if you're just getting started then somebody's eventually going to ask what justifies your arrogance. So just be yourself. Trying to act like one of those industry stereotypes will send an artist running for her copy of "So You Want to Be a Rock-and-Roll Star" for anti-establishment comfort.

If you are approaching someone unsolicited, lay all your cards on the table. Acknowledge that you are meeting the person unsolicited and that you are even a little apprehensive about doing so, worried that you may give them the wrong impression. Behaving like an honest, trustworthy human being who is temporarily a bit shy will both puncture this slimy bubble and establish an eye-to-eye connection. A hidden upside to this is that if you are always straight with a prospective client and they don't like you and decide not to work with you, then you're both better off. Neither party benefits from working with someone who doesn't genuinely want to work with the other. Engines work best when all pistons are firing.

Be sure to be clear that you are approaching someone because you think they're great. You admire the person's talent, but you don't necessarily want to exploit that talent. What you want is to have the person use *you* to help further their musical career. You are their tool for success, not the other way around. But just don't act like a tool.

My first unsolicited signing was a band from St. Paul, Minnesota, called Look Down. I'd been a big fan of theirs for years and they were getting some pretty large crowds in their hometown. They were fantastic: wrote great songs, were totally at ease and charismatic onstage, and seemed like they were ready to make the jump. Until I introduced myself to Look Down, Afternoon Records' releases had been by my own band, Aneuretical, and by bands led by some of my friends. So it was particularly nerve-racking and intimidating to approach a band of strangers.

It was my first time, and I was a bit clumsy. This is how it went down. They had just finished playing a sold-out show at Eclipse Records in St. Paul, and I approached them as they were packing up their gear. After a few Hey!s, I finally snagged the lead singer Jacob Huelster's attention as he was packing up his bass.

"Hey, I'm Ian."

"Hey, Ian."

"I like your band."

"That's cool, man."

"Listen, I run a label and I want to put your record out."

"Really? How old are you?"

"Eighteen."

"Funny. Yeah, here's my number."

I know those words look like magic and that no one could possibly be as smooth as that, but that's how it happened. Apply dating protocol to courting bands and you'll hit the right tone, oddly enough. I waited a few days to call and nervously picked up the torn piece of paper that had Jacob's number on it. I felt a lot like Kevin from *The Wonder Years* calling Winnie Cooper, and dialed.

The band and I met the next weekend at a coffee shop. Here is a key point: meet somewhere public and relaxed. Inviting a band to an office can often feel intimidating to them, so find a common, neutral ground that will make things a bit more comfortable.

"So what do you do?" they asked.

"Not really that much, yet. But I'm learning fast."

"Well, why should we sign with you, then?"

"I'll record the record myself in my studio for free, pay for manufacturing, put it in stores, promote it to local papers, and try to send you on tour."

"Cool, are you going to dick us?"

"What?"

"Are you going to screw us over?"

"No."

"All right, no one else wants to sign us, so deal."

Jacob always had a very matter-of-fact way of dealing with things, which I liked. We then spent the next two months working in a buddy's studio and released their *The American Hustle* EP a month after that.

The main point to take from this exchange? Brutal honesty can work for you. I admitted to them that I didn't have a whole lot to offer, but that I was hungry and eager. They admitted they didn't have any other options, so why not try me?

That's one success story, but I've had my share of blunders. When I tried to sign the band Morris, also awesome, they flat-out asked for details about my distribution capabilities. I was honest and explained that I did it myself over the phone and had no distribution deal with a larger company. They promptly said no. I later found out that they thought I wasn't cool. Well, ouch, but ultimately that worked out fine because they wanted distribution, which I couldn't provide. Also, I didn't want to work with a band that didn't think I was cool. Just kidding. Most bands don't think I'm cool.

After a few encounters and perhaps a small blunder or two, you'll begin to develop an effective and professional meeting vibe. It just takes time and experience. I was very nervous for my first dozen or so tries at this, but then I started to develop a knack for figuring out what bands want to know from me and how.I can answer their questions in a clear, unintimidating, and unintimidated manner. But on the bright side, you won't have to approach people forever. Artists and bands will eventually start coming to you if you do a good job.

Which leads me to my most important point: always do a good job. Doing your best is crucial to gaining the support of local music media, to building contacts within your local music community, and to developing and maintaining a solid reputation that will pave the way ahead of you in future dealings with bands you'll meet. You must always work hard and try your damnedest to fulfill the obligations in your agreements with artists. No slacking, no excuses.

Some artists might complain that I haven't made them into the next Nirvana, but they absolutely know I tried my hardest and gave it my best effort. If you do your best, more often than not things will turn out well, because hard work achieves results. Sure, some releases are destined to stay on the shelves—that's just the roll of the dice—but you always need to try.

I hope you're listening. Reputation is critical in the music industry. If you come off as lazy or flat-out incompetent to a client, he or she will report your poor performance to others. So you must move heaven and earth and a few mountains to make sure that you are always putting your best foot forward and are producing your best work at all times. It seems like a lot of pressure, but it is simply the truth.

10

Manufacturing

Now that you know who you are, know what record you are going to release, have already recorded it, and know how you're going to create revenue once it is released, you need to actually make those LPs!

The first thing you need to understand is that what you are releasing is, in fact, a product. It's a product that you are going to introduce into the marketplace. You are running a business just like any other business: you create a product for which you think there's a demand, you make that product accessible to the public for purchase, and if there is truly demand for your product, then you've done something right and it will sell. The artist, the LP, and live performances are all products that you have to sell. Products, marketplace, selling—maybe that doesn't square in your head with art, artists, and music, but try to make peace between those ideas. Making music work as a business is what allows it to be shared as art.

The first thing to recognize about a great product is that it must look as great on the outside as it sounds inside. Great-looking artwork is vital to a successful release. You might have a lot of art-school friends who would "totally do it for free." I do, too, and they're nice kids, but they are *not* professionals. You will get out of a project what you put into it, so if it's possible, spring for great artwork. Remember, if you are working with a great band that has made a great record, you want the artwork to accurately represent that awesome recording just as much as you want that awesome recording to represent that killer band. Take a look around. Read the liner notes in your favorite albums to find out who designed them. Check out design firms and coalitions in your area. Go to art galleries, read art magazines, ask around about designers, find those designers, then ask about other designers they know. It's a long process and will remind you of what it took to find your lawyer, but all that legwork will get you somewhere in the end. Remember, finding someone who can share in your vision and the direction of the label and the band is the priority here. Don't settle for something else.

Once you have a visual artist on deck to do the artwork, you must find a manufacturing company and arrange delivery of the finished album art to them. Part of that conversation includes negotiating the format in which they want to receive this: file type, size, on what template, etc. Every manufacturing company worth a hill of beans has all this listed on their website in plain and simple terms. Generally, files are delivered on a CDR or are uploaded to the manufacturer's server as .tiff files at a resolution of 300 dpi (dots per inch).

That covers the art; however, the audio is different. Your mastering engineer will know what to do. The manufacturer will want a reference master, which is often called a *glass master*, a term that originated back when masters were actually made of glass (they no longer are). This is basically the "final copy" of the record, which consists of the final .wav or .aiff files for each track in the correct order and with the correct spacing between tracks. With both those items turned in to the manufacturer, you can take the next step.

Since you are starting small, you'll have to place some constraints on your manufacturing flexibility. For instance, you should manufacture only a thousand copies and have only a two-panel CD insert (no booklet and just one sheet of paper as an insert). You'll economize with jewel cases instead of digipaks to keep the costs down. You'll earmark five hundred copies for retail (and you'll direct the manufacturing company to shrink-wrap these copies with a top spine and an intact barcode—the barcode can be provided by the manufacturer and should be placed in one of the corners on the back of the CD) and five hundred copies for promotion (these will be unwrapped, with a punched barcode). I'll explain more about why these differ later. Most CD manufacturing plants can get this done for you in about two weeks and for about $1,300. I strongly recommend that you take the time to get a sample product from the plant. Some manufacturing companies use flimsy and easily breakable materials to keep costs down. You don't want to be surprised, and you don't want your artists to be unhappily surprised, and poor-quality CDs do not create an image that you want. My next recommendation is optional, but I always like to ask a manufacturing company in advance where they get their materials and where they outsource anything they don't do. I like to make sure they don't use sweatshops or any shady means to manufacture CDs.

One company I have always been very fond of is Noiseland Industries (www.noiselandindustries.com): they are a Minneapolis-based company that uses strong, well-made, and well-designed materials that always look great. I can call them at any time with any sort of manufacturing time-crunch emergency and they'll work it out with me—and by now, they even recognize my voice on the phone, which is undeniably cool. No, I don't get a cut of their business. But I hope you can find a company in your region that is as steadfast and responsible. Ask around, talk to other labels, find out who is trustworthy. It is important to find a company that you can trust and that makes you feel comfortable. You're a business, you'll be sending them work, so you should develop a good relationship with them. A first-name basis is by no means out of the question.

A few companies that I have worked with in the past have done some dreadful work, forgetting about a project, missing deadlines, not getting back to me with answers to my questions—not to mention making shoddy products. Responsibility, follow-through, responsiveness, and competence are reasonable things to expect from a manufacturing company. Be sure you get them.

I recommend that you think locally. If you can work with a company that is just down the street, troubleshooting becomes person-to-person if you ever encounter a snafu, and pickup and shipping becomes almost a nonissue.

If you can't find a solid local company, then any company in the country is open to you. In this case, thoroughly scout out your prospects. One, because you now have so many options. And two, because you'll need to trust these folks long-distance, so you need to feel confident they'll be responsive to you. Ask for samples and get quotes from at least three companies for every project.

On average, you'll pay about $1.30 for one CD—maybe $1.00 for larger quantities. Some companies are significantly more expensive, some are a lot less, but around a buck a CD is truly the middle ground. I am wary of companies who charge $880 for a thousand CDs because I wonder what they are using as manufacturing materials. To pass that savings on to you, they must be cutting a corner or two somewhere, and I want to know what those corners are. Ask questions; the answers might satisfy you and you might just have found an inexpensive manufacturer. And if you're quoted $1,500 for a thousand CDs, ask why they are so expensive. There might be a special material being used, or the company might be trying to take advantage of you.

One note about planning. Figure on manufacturing taking about two weeks, and prepare your marketing plans and adjust your artists' expectations accordingly.

Vinyl

Manufacturing vinyl is a whole other story. It is a much longer process (three-months-ish), so be sure to start it early. There are only a few manufacturing plants in the United States that make things easy: they are United, R.T.I., and Pirates Press. An entirely separate master needs to be produced in order to manufacture vinyl records. Be sure to ask for test pressings so you can listen before you pull the manufacturing trigger. Artwork ostensibly costs the same, but is just bigger. The costs are higher—about $3 a unit as opposed to $1 for CDs—but it is often worth it, because vinyl is just so great.

11

Distribution

Distribution is the process by which records are placed in stores. Once the manufacturer delivers finished CDs to you, then the trip the CDs take from you to retailers to consumers is called *distribution*.

Local Distribution

Be it on the local, regional, national, or even international level, most distribution networks start at the same point: your car. You need to know every record store, both the independents and the chains, in your neighborhood, in your city, perhaps even in your region. And your car needs to know the way to get there.

Before you ever release a record, you need to talk to your local record stores. At each shop, you need to learn the name and contact information of whoever you will talk to there in order to get your releases on their shelves. Start keeping a notebook, store this stuff in your PDA, carry your laptop into stores, whatever is your style. But make like a businessperson: identify your targets (stores) and get to know the people who can buy product from you. Build relationships. Stop in now and then even before you have records to sell. Get to know the staff. Talk about what you're doing. Get them excited for that first day when you walk in carrying a cardboard box of CDs.

When you chat with store owners, you want to learn about them, about the stores they run, and about what they like and how they like it. Do they like one-sheets or other promotional materials with every release? Do they want promo copies? Posters? Maybe even guest-list spots at local shows? The first time you sit down with a local record store owner, he or she is likely to ask to sell your records on consignment. Consignment isn't the greatest option in the world for you, but it does ensure that your albums are on the shelves—and it's a start.

Consignment

Consignment is a situation in which you get your CD on the shelves of a record store without the store having to buy the record from you initially. This will most likely be the first step to get your records in stores, because it is a low-risk venture for stores themselves. You sign a minicontract (this could be as complex as a three- or four-page form or as primitive as a handwritten slip of paper) that specifies how much you need from each sale. Then the store marks up the price anywhere from 30 to 50 percent. For a full-length CD, you want $8 to $10; on consignment, that means the store will sell it from $12.99 to $14.99. Since you're brand-new, you might use a strategy of shooting for the cheaper end of things. Take $8 a CD and let the record store mark it up to $12.99.

Critical to the success of working a consignment deal: remember to check in with the store on a monthly or bimonthly basis to see how things are moving. This helps you cement your relationship with them, which is a good thing, and also lets you know quickly if the shop needs more copies. Most local stores are pretty good about contacting the label if they've sold out of a release, but there will always be one or two shops that continually neglect this task. That makes it worth your while to check in.

Load up the car and hit the road.

Direct Wholesale

Other than consignment, you may sometimes get the option of having a store order from you directly on a wholesale basis. This means they buy the record from you outright and sell it for whatever price they like. This is the most desirable distribution situation in many ways, but it has a few complications. Granted, you have your $8 up front. However, a store buying from you at wholesale will most likely buy only a copy or two. If you consign the release, you can put as many copies as you like (or that each store will allow) on the shelves.

Another wholesale challenge is simply getting paid in a timely manner for your product. If you work with a distributor, your distributor can also go to bat for you and help you get your money. However, as a new little label, you have to do your own negotiating and nagging. That's why working with a distributor can be the most ideal distribution situation. For instance, if a store a thousand miles away from you decides not to pay you for one copy of one release, it really isn't that big a deal to them, because (a) you don't really have much power of persuasion when they are so far away, and (b) they may never order from you again, so you have nothing to use as collateral, although you could refrain from filling future orders until you are paid for the previous ones. This is where a distributor wins. They have many titles and are most likely working with the same stores every week, so any given store will never want to risk bruising that relationship by delaying payment excessively.

One-Stops—A Level Up

A one-stop is the next step. Let's say you've been networking well with a web of local shops, and have been selling so many records that it becomes difficult for you to keep up with all your various consignments. Now you must seek out and upgrade to what is called a one-stop. A one-stop is a sort of minidistributor for a specific region. A one-stop passes along records from larger distributors or from record labels to stores. If you can get in with the local one-stop in your area, then you can bypass most of the local consignment and you'll rack up fewer miles on that poor car.

One-stops are arguably the most effective way to get your records into smaller independent stores. Since most smaller stores don't have huge budgets at their disposal, they often prefer to buy just one or two copies of an album at a time, and one-stops allow them to do that. One-stops can offer flexible terms of payment to stores and often set up sixty- to ninety-day pay cushions that allow stores to pay for what they have sold, or to return what they haven't sold, by the end of the payment period. Although this is a very kindhearted service to provide to indie stores, it does pose a problem to distributors and to labels like yours who would like to get paid in a timely fashion and do not want to wait ninety days or more to see turnaround results on a release. Oftentimes this is how cash flow problems begin.

Independent Distribution

Things work very differently through a distributor, however—the pie gets divided a few more times. When an independent distributor picks you up, they will most likely place an order for thirty copies of an album initially and will "pay" you $5 to $7 per unit. (I put *pay* in quotation marks because most independent distributors do not pay upfront and will send you a check long after sales have happened). This is far less than what you get on consignment at your local store. The trade-off is this: a distributor does the legwork of contacting stores and talking to them about your releases. Rather than paying them up front like a publicist or a promoter, you pay them on commission (about 20 percent of each unit they sell). Once you add that 20 percent to the 30 to 50 percent the store is already taking, only the leftover $5 to $7 is what you get in the end. When your strategy is above all to get the releases into stores, you may choose to accept these lower profits.

Now knowing what you are getting yourself into, how do you get into it? Currently, there are roughly fifty well-established and substantial independent distributors in the United States. Each has their own niche and each has their own special way of running things. However, they have some general characteristics in common. Landing a distributor is a lot like getting a bank loan. In order to get a bank loan, you have to prove that you don't need the money. When it comes to distribution, you want to look like you don't need help selling records. If you can sell records steadily and consistently on your own without the aid of any bigger fish, then those big fish get interested in helping you. My advice: make opportunities for distributors to become aware of you, and, in the end, let them come to you.

Let distributors learn about you by sending them every Thank-you Records release for review. If they are interested, they'll call you.

A few years into the life of Thankyou Records, you will, ideally, have a track record that makes you worthy of working with many distributors. Once you get to that point, you will coordinate with a handful of distribution companies to ensure that you are in most, if not all, markets. Each distributor tends to work within a specific region, and stores often prefer certain distributors over others. So if you are being distributed by Southern in the Southeast United States, and Carrot Top in the Northeast and Midwest, you must connect with other distributors that will help get you west of the Mississippi River.

Direct Distribution: What If No One Calls?

If no one calls, you'll have yourself a little cry and then pull yourself together. You wouldn't be reading this book if you weren't a pretty strong and independent person in the other areas of your life, so steel yourself for a bit of rejection now and then. Distribution is a lot of work and sure, we'd all love some help. But if it doesn't happen, you'll figure it out, because that's what independent record labels do: figure it out.

Working without a distributor, it becomes even more important to have a solid and well-developed network of independent record stores, record-store coalitions, and one-stops. Then you work that base, calling, visiting, and talking to their representatives at events, and keeping yourself at the forefront—all this works to remind them that they can get your records through you directly. There are a few ways to truly accomplish this, and I recommend you do a bit of everything:

1. Compile a list of every record store you can locate.
2. Call them, e-mail them, or carrier-pigeon them, letting them know that you exist and really want to work with them.
3. Follow up with them by sending press kits of your bands. Make it extremely easy for them to learn about you and listen to the music that you are putting out.
4. Do these things every week.
5. The most badass option: visit every store on your list.

All those options are doable. They just take a lot of time and effort. Does number five look a little tricky? Come on, you love hanging out at record stores. The stores that will work with you the most will be the ones you've made a personal connection with, the ones in which shop owners have seen your smiling face and shaken your hand. One of the great side benefits of touring with my band, One for the Team, is that I travel all over the United States, so I can more easily meet with more record store owners. You may not have a band of your own or that luxury—but you can still make the most of any travel you do. Find record stores wherever you go and hit them—at least the big ones. Make a list of the ten most important record stores in your distribution network and set up a meeting with their owners. Drive, fly, swim, or just hike to each store. You'd be surprised at how many labels don't bother. This will set you apart and make you easier to remember.

The Cake Shop in New York City is one of my favorite record stores in the country, and they really know it. The Cake Shop is a coffee-and-dessert-music-venue-record-store hybrid on the Lower East Side of Manhattan. I fell in love with it when I first stumbled upon it during the CMJ Music Festival in 2003. I walked in and thought, *This is the greatest record store I have ever seen.* It is beyond small, with barely ten square feet of standing room, but it has a surprisingly diverse and consistently great selection, composed with the unassailably cool music taste of the store's owner, Andy Bodor. I immediately introduced myself to him and eagerly thrust a compilation disc of Afternoon Records titles into his hand, practically pleading with him to give my roster a listen. Each time I visited New York after that first contact, I made it a point to stop in and bug him a little, some dozen times over the next three years. Eventually, Andy came to recognize me. Granted, he recognized me as that annoying kid from Minnesota who had his own label, but it was recognition, nonetheless. Eventually the Cake Shop started carrying my records and hosting Afternoon Records bands to play there. The extra effort definitely worked.

There are two primary coalitions of independent record stores in the United States: the Alliance of Independent Music Stores (AIMS), and the Coalition of Independent Music Stores (CIMS). Both comprise larger independent stores throughout the United States that share similar outlooks on style, music, and tastemaking. It is crucial to tap into these groups of stores when you push a record, because if one of them picks up a release, chances are, the others will get interested too.

Making This All Connect

Now that we know where your records need to go, how do you make it happen?

Since you chose to produce only five hundred CDs for retail for your first release, you should ration out your distribution wisely. Here's a good breakdown for two different situations:

WITH A DISTRIBUTION DEAL FOR NATIONAL STORES:
100 for the band to sell on their own at shows
100 for local stores
200 for national distribution
50 for online sales through your website
50 for restock

WITHOUT A DISTRIBUTION DEAL FOR NATIONAL STORES:
200 for the band to sell on their own
150 for local stores
100 for online sales through your website
50 for restock

It doesn't feel like much to spread around, because it's not. But that's what a repress is for—and I'll get to that later.

Strategic Distribution

Simply put: go where your clients are. Don't spend the time and effort to get a store in Ann Arbor, Michigan, to pick up your record if you don't think anyone will actually go into that store looking for it. That said, you might be surprised where your bands find fans. Fans can come out of the woodwork from every nook and cranny of the world, bless them! But with only five hundred CDs, you need to make these decisions carefully.

There are specific methods you can use to make the most informed decisions possible about where to place your CDs. The first method is the easiest and cheapest because it's free: create and use a mailing/e-mail list. At your shows and on your website, provide an opportunity for fans to sign up for label and artist updates. When these fine people sign up, be sure to ask where they live. Suddenly, you have a piece of valuable demographic information. If one person signs up from Duluth, Minnesota, you love that guy but may not choose to tour your bands there. But if thirty-seven people sign up from Sioux Falls, South Dakota, suddenly you have a lot of motivation to get your bands out to Sioux Falls, and make sure that your releases are in stores in and around Sioux Falls.

Distribution Deals

Back in the mid-1990s, distribution deals worked like this: a label got a call from a bigger label or a distribution company offering a *pressing and distribution deal*, or a *P&D*. Under a P&D, the larger company manufactured a small label's CDs and then "bought" them at a wholesale price. The larger company also vended out the CD to retailers. A smaller label wouldn't have to drop a penny on manufacturing anything, but it was also paid only the wholesale price by the distributor.

Today, deals work a bit more informally because the industry doesn't generate as much revenue as it used to—revenue that allowed for this kind of risk-taking deal to be made. If Thankyou Records got a call today from a distribution company, it would sound more like receiving a large store order. If Carrot Top Distribution were on the other line, they might order thirty copies of a single release as a test run, and if those sell, they may order another thirty later.

We can understand a distribution company's cold feet. Would you really want to take a risk on ordering and paying for more than thirty copies of an unknown artist's release on an unknown label? Probably not. So count your lucky stars and consider yourself fortunate that you even got the call in the first place, and do whatever you can to help move those thirty units that were just ordered.

Lying outside deals with distribution companies are subdistribution deals. Although these are hard to come by, they do happen. Thankyou Records might sign a deal with a bigger label, like Saddle Creek or Matador Records. Such a label, in turn, then becomes the sole distributor of the Thankyou Records catalog. This is sometimes called "upstreaming" to a larger label; a bigger fish is being nice and is taking you under its distribution network's wing—or fin in this case—and is fulfilling your distribution needs by distributing your product through their channels.

Generally, these deals are a no-brainer. If you need distribution, you just need it, and you take what you can get. However, in upstreaming you will lose anywhere from 20 to 30 percent of retail sale to that bigger fish. In the end, that leaves you with little revenue after the store, the distributor, and the bigger fish/label divide up the pie.

Another downside to upstreaming is that you may simply be treated like a second-class citizen by the higher-ups in a bigger company, and therefore may find yourself not the priority. Obviously, you are a bit lower on the food chain and therefore your name will be similarly situated lower on the priority list.

Placement and Co-ops

Particular placement of records on the shelves in priority spots—at eye level or on endcaps (the prominent CD rack at the end of the shopping aisle)—is valuable. Shops charge a fee to place a record in a specific spot in a specific store; that fee is called a co-op. For example, if it costs you a $5,000 co-op to get the Readers' first CD into prime locations in fifty different Starbucks locations, Starbucks takes 40 percent of each sale, and your distributor takes another 30 percent, you may get only $5 or less per CD sold—and you're also out the additional $5,000 it took to get you there. You need to sell at least a thousand copies in Starbucks alone just to break even. Furthermore, to properly stock those fifty locations, Starbucks may ask for five copies of the album for each store—however, each store will need to sell an average of twenty CDs for you to meet your goal of breaking even. So ship five to each store, and hang on to the other fifteen in your closet in hopes that the original five will sell through and Starbucks will order more. Therefore you end up blocking off a thousand copies of the Readers' CD when that is all you could afford to manufacture in the first place.

Let's pretend for a moment that you actually do have the resources to make the Starbucks deal happen. Everything is running smoothly, you have the initial $5,000 to buy the shelf space, you manufacture more than enough CDs, and you're ready to go with restock. Then disaster strikes and you sell only one album per store. The end of your deal period approaches and Starbucks comes to you with only fifty album sales and an extended hand waiting for that $5,000 check. Not only did you lose money, but you cost Starbucks money too. They allocated that shelf space to a dud. They have your $5,000, but they would have had more money, their 40 percent per sale, had your product moved. You will not be offered this deal again for some time—if ever.

So the moral of the story is, do not stretch beyond your means. Start small and stay small until you have no other option than to get bigger.

12

Digital Distribution

Digital distribution is likely the most important form of product placement for growing young record labels. What the future standard medium for music will be, and what the future methods of distribution of music will be, are completely up in the air. Add that to an ever growing proliferation of downloadable music websites, and it's reasonable for all music label owners to stay flexible and agile in choosing the distribution systems we use.

You need to know about the distribution systems I've already discussed because there may be years when you need to straddle two worlds. I want you prepped and ready for both of them. Music fans may shift totally to digital downloads, and physical CDs in cases may become rare. On the other hand, think about books: some people like to read for hours online and other people want that solid book in their hands. And hey—no one thought vinyl was ever coming back. So widen your options and be ready to move in whatever direction best suits your mission—or maybe move in all directions.

Undoubtedly, independents have many reasons to love digital: its low cost, its speed, its accessibility to fans who live anywhere.

IODA and CD Baby

Here is where we start.

IODA (the Independent Online Distribution Alliance) and CD Baby are arguably the best independent online download distributors available to independent record labels. At this point (2009), iTunes is the largest U.S. music retailer and will most likely remain so for some time, not only because iTunes has the best and easiest download interface, but also because Apple acts aggressively to set consumer trends in the digital market. Outside iTunes, Amazon and eMusic are my personal favorites. These are all essential avenues for distribution. As the nature of music sales evolves, these may be *the* avenues (although I still collect vinyl, and I bet you do too).

To go digital, we need to plan in advance. First, pick one digital distributor and get registered with it. Say you choose IODA and contact the artist representatives there. Expect the back-and-forth discussions about what you want to distribute through them and how they want to work with you to take about three months. (See what I mean? *Advance* planning!)

The key questions you'll want to have answered: (a) Where are your MP3s going? (b) How will they get there? (c) Under what kind of deal will they arrive? and (d) How do you protect yourself as the copyright owner of these musical works?

Once you've established a working relationship, you will send a promotional copy of your newest release with a one-sheet. When your digital distributor receives your record, they will begin to process the release. This means that they upload the audio files, artwork, song title information, copyright information, and publishing materials to their server, and then distribute that information to all their digital outlets.

ISRC Registrant Code

Now you register with the RIAA (Recording Industry Association of America) to get an ISRC registrant code for your label. This is how you'll get paid. It's a quick and painless process at www.riaa.com.

An ISRC (International Standard Recording Code) works in a manner somewhat similar to how barcodes work with actual CD hard copies, except that they are associated with individual tracks and are embedded in the .mp3, .aiff, .flac, .wav, and other file versions of each. Think of the ISRC as a digitally embedded barcode in each audio file.

Let's say you're registering the first single of the Readers' CD. Here is what the ISRC code would look like: US-TYR-09-00101

The first two characters (US) of the ISRC represent the country code, which in our case is the United States.

The second batch (TYR) is the registrant code, which represents the label that is releasing the music, Thankyou Records (TYR).

The next two digits represent the year-of-reference code, which is 09 for 2009, or the year in which the music was released.

The last five characters are the designation code, or the code that you have assigned to the individual track to represent it uniquely. I picked the first three digits as your release number (001, your first release) and the last two digits as the track number of the song on the album (01, the first track, your hot single).

Now that we've protected our tracks with ISRCs, what exactly will the IODA do with our digital tracks? They function just like any other distributor. Just as a hard-copy distributor contacts each retailer in its network and pitches the record to each shop, our digital distributor takes our release and sends it out to every digital retailer in its network. But rather than sending 1,000 or 2,500 hard CDs to stores, they simply upload the files to various servers owned by each retailer. Pretty neat, huh?

Deals with Amazon and iTunes

Deals with different digital distributors work in all sorts of crazy ways. The most straightforward deals come from the likes of Amazon and iTunes. Here's what they look like; my translations follow.

Amazon Digital Download Deal Summary

Usage.
Full Length Digital Download MP3 Format

ALBUMS with 10 or more Tracks, where the Metadata indicates the number of discs to be one, "Standard Album":

PRICE CODE (TIER)	ALBUM WHOLESALE	TRACK WHOLESALE
FRONTLINE	$6.50	$0.70
MIDLINE	$5.60	$0.63
CATALOG	$4.90	$0.63
SPECIAL	$4.00	$0.63

ALBUMS and EPs with less than 10 Tracks:

For Albums with less than 10 tracks, and where one or more track(s) on the Album are designated "Album Only," the Standard Album Price Codes noted above adhere.

For Albums with less than 10 tracks and where no tracks are designated "Album Only," the Albums (both ALBUMS and EPs) shall be priced as below.

PRICE CODE (TIER)	ALBUM WHOLESALE	TRACK WHOLESALE
FRONTLINE 9 tracks	$6.12	$0.70
FRONTLINE 8 tracks	$5.44	$0.70
FRONTLINE 7 tracks	$4.76	$0.70
FRONTLINE 6 tracks	$4.08	$0.70
FRONTLINE 5 tracks	$3.40	$0.70
FRONTLINE 4 tracks	$2.72	$0.70
FRONTLINE 3 tracks	$2.04	$0.70
FRONTLINE 2 tracks	$1.36	$0.70

(Albums with 1 track are qualified as SINGLES)

	ALBUM WHOLESALE	TRACK WHOLESALE
MIDLINE 9 tracks	$5.60	$0.63
MIDLINE 8 tracks	$5.04	$0.63
MIDLINE 7 tracks	$4.41	$0.63
MIDLINE 6 tracks	$3.78	$0.63

MIDLINE 5 tracks	$3.15	$0.63
MIDLINE 4 tracks	$2.52	$0.63
MIDLINE 3 tracks	$1.89	$0.63
MIDLINE 2 tracks	$1.26	$0.63

(Albums with 1 track are qualified as SINGLES)

CATALOG 9 tracks	$4.90	$0.63
CATALOG 8 tracks	$4.90	$0.63
CATALOG 7 tracks	$4.41	$0.63
CATALOG 6 tracks	$3.78	$0.63
CATALOG 5 tracks	$3.15	$0.63
CATALOG 4 tracks	$2.52	$0.63
CATALOG 3 tracks	$1.89	$0.63
CATALOG 2 tracks	$1.26	$0.63

(Albums with 1 track are qualified as SINGLES)

SPECIAL 7–9 tracks	$4.00	$0.63
SPECIAL 6 tracks	$3.78	$0.63
SPECIAL 5 tracks	$3.15	$0.63
SPECIAL 4 tracks	$2.52	$0.63
SPECIAL 3 tracks	$1.89	$0.63
SPECIAL 2 tracks	$1.26	$0.63

(Albums with 1 track are qualified as SINGLES)

SINGLES.

The wholesale price for SINGLES (provided as an Album with a single track on it) shall adhere to the following:

PRICE CODE (TIER)	TRACK WHOLESALE
FRONTLINE	$0.70
MIDLINE	$0.63
CATALOG	$0.63
SPECIAL	$0.63

Multi-Album Pricing.

If the Metadata indicates that the Number of Discs for a particular Album is two, then the wholesale price for that Album will be double the Standard Album wholesale price indicated above for the corresponding Price Code. If the Metadata indicates that the Number of Discs for a particular Album is three or more, then the wholesale price for that Album will be double the Standard Album wholesale price indicated above for the corresponding Price Code unless the Price Code is set to CUSTOM, in which case the wholesale price will be the amount indicated in Price Override field.

Publishing.

IODA Labels are responsible for securing mechanical licenses, and paying all associated fees and royalties for sales in the United States.

Public Performance licenses are not the responsibility of IODA Labels.

Territory.

United States

Term.

One (1) year Term that extends for a period of 12 months from the earlier of: (a) the date the service commences commercial distribution; and (b) _____ ___, _____. The Term automatically renews for successive 1 year periods unless either party provides the other party with at least 60 days notice of nonrenewal.

Reporting/Payment.

Amazon will issue statements and corresponding payments 45 days after the calendar month; provided, however, that Amazon shall retain the right in its discretion to determine that the first statement hereunder shall be issued 45 days after the end of the calendar month that includes the date that is 60 days following the launch of the service for transactions occurring up to the end of such month.

What we're looking at here is pretty standard. For "Frontline" albums, Amazon will sell each track for $.99 and will pay IODA

$.70 for each track downloaded by a customer. IODA will then take 15 percent off the $.70, which results in our receiving $.605 per download. Not so bad, considering that we are only submitting the music and have basically no overhead costs for this form of our product.

In this deal, wholesale purchases work a little bit differently. If a customer downloads an entire album in one fell swoop, Amazon pays IODA $6.50. Amazon is trying to undercut iTunes by selling full-length albums for $8.90 instead of iTunes's $9.99. In the end, after the pie is divided, we receive $5.52 per album purchased at wholesale.

Let's look at how iTunes compares.

iTunes U.S./Canada Deal Summary

Usage.
Single tracks, Multi-Track Albums, and Videos
Rate.
iTunes agrees to pay IODA the following Wholesale Prices:

Single tracks (excluding taxes):

REGULAR EMASTER	PLUS EMASTER	UPGRADE*
US $0.70	Greater of 70 percent retail price (excluding taxes) or US $0.70 floor wholesale price	US $0.20
CDN $0.70	Greater of 70 percent retail price (excluding taxes) or CDN $0.70 floor wholesale price	CDN $0.26

*The first sale of a particular single-track Plus eMaster to an end user who previously purchased the same single track from the Online Store as a Regular eMaster shall be deemed an Upgrade.

Multi-Track Albums (excluding taxes):

ALBUM TIERS	REGULAR/PLUS ALBUM	ALBUM UPGRADE*
Mini-EP	US $1.40	US $0.40
	CDN $1.65	CDN $0.41
EP	US $2.80	US $0.80
	CDN $2.80	CDN $0.70
Budget	US $4.20	US $1.20
	CDN $4.20	CDN $1.05
Back	US $5.60	US $1.60
	CDN $5.60	CDN $1.40
Mid/Front	US $7.00	US $2.00
	CDN $7.00	CDN $1.75
Front Plus	US $8.40	US $2.40
	CDN $8.40	CDN $2.10
Multi-CD Sets	(Selected Album Tier Wholesale Price) x (# of CDs)	(Selected Album Tier Wholesale Price) x (# of CDs)

The Wholesale price for any multi-track album shall not exceed the aggregate price of the single tracks on that album if sold separately as single tracks.

Single Videos

REGULAR/PLUS EMASTER	VIDEO UPGRADE**
US $1.40	US $0.40
CDN $1.65	CDN $0.52 excluding taxes

---

*The first sale of a particular multi-track album in Plus eMaster format to an end user who previously purchased the same multi-track album from the Online Store in Regular eMaster format shall be deemed an Album Upgrade.

**The first sale of a particular single-video Plus eMaster to an end user who previously purchased the same single video from the Online Store as a Regular eMaster shall be deemed a Video Upgrade.

Rate and Revenue Calculation.

	PERCENT RETAIL	SINGLE TRACK US	MID FRONT ALBUM US	SINGLE TRACK CANADA	MID FRONT ALBUM CANADA
Retail Price	100 percent	US $0.99	US $9.99	CDN $0.99	CDN $9.99
iTunes Share	30 percent	US $0.29	US $2.99	CDN $0.29	CDN $2.99
IODA/Label Share	70 percent	US $0.70	US $7.00	CDN $0.70	CDN $7.00

Publishing; Audio.

United States
Mechanical Licenses. IODA Labels are responsible for securing mechanical licenses, and paying all associated fees and royalties for sales in the United States.

Performance Licenses. IODA Labels are not responsible for securing public performance licenses, and paying all associated fees and royalties, if applicable, for sales in the United States.

Canada
Tracks that can be cleared through CMRRA-SODRAC:

iTunes shall be responsible for obtaining mechanical and public performance rights for musical compositions and for paying the associated fees for label content for which reproduction rights in Canada may be cleared and paid through CMRRA-SODRAC, Inc ("CSI"); iTunes shall make such payments only to CMRRA-SODRAC, Inc., and to no other party.

Tracks that cannot be cleared through CMRRA-SODRAC:

IODA Labels will be solely responsible for all musical composition rights and associated payments for all audio-only full-length content sold in Canada that is not registered with CMRRA-SODRAC. IODA labels should consult with the owner or controller of the musical compositions to identify which musical compositions are registered with CMRRA-SODRAC. Please note that the wholesale prices paid to IODA Labels are the same regardless of whether or not IODA Labels are responsible for the musical composition licenses.

Royalty Rate Reduction:
Canadian Rates reflect a deduction for musical composition rights based on industry-wide royalty rates, currently estimated at eight percent (8 percent) of retail price. Wholesale prices may be prospectively reduced or increased if higher or lower prevailing industry-wide royalty rates are established by a court, tribunal within the Territory, or through negotiations.

Publishing; Video.

Mechanical Licenses
United States and Canada: IODA Labels are responsible for securing mechanical licenses and paying all associated fees.

Performance Licenses
United States and Canada: IODA Labels are not responsible for securing public performance licenses or paying the associated fees.

Territory.
United States and Canada.
Term.
Three (3) year Term commencing on _____ and ending on _____, and automatically renewing thereafter for additional three-year periods until terminated by either party upon ninety (90) days' written notice.
Reporting/Payment.
iTunes will issue and make available Sales Reports and corresponding payments to IODA after the end of each monthly period during the Term.

Just like Amazon, iTunes pays IODA $.70 per download but pays $7.00 per wholesale purchase. You cannot afford to not be on either of these sites, in the same way that the major labels can't afford not to be in Best Buy and Target. So you must accept the reality that you won't see the fullest retail value of your product. Five years from now, iTunes and Amazon will still be the places where most music is sold, so I'd suggest accustoming yourself to them now.

Importance

Immediate gratification is what these avenues really provide. And that is really what our generation of consumers wants: the ability to visit a handful of blogs daily, find something they like and, in less than five clicks, own the song or the entire album. So how do we market in this kind of fast-consumption culture? I'll address that in chapter 16, "Getting the Word Out," under my discussion of blog campaigns.

Diversification of Digital Content

When it comes to digital retail, consumer loyalty exists just as much as it does with brick-and-mortar stores, and for the same reasons.

A 2008 study by the NPD Group, a leading market researcher, found that only 10 percent of Amazon's MP3 buyers had ever used iTunes (see www.npd.com/press/releases/press_080415.html). This is a staggering bit of marketing knowledge. For one thing, it reinforces my conviction that you had better distribute digitally to both Amazon *and* iTunes—there isn't much crossover. For another, it means that the digital market has room to grow—all those digital customers over at iTunes haven't gotten comfortable with Amazon yet, and vice versa.

Plus, certain digital retailers do cater to different digital demographics. There is not a single online music marketplace that you go to—and so does your mother. Instead, there are many online music markets that are suited to individual market niches (specific combinations of age, taste, region, etc.). That is the beauty of the Internet, after all. It's capable of almost infinite individualization when it comes to the marketplace.

Think of selling your music on a new site as if you were building a new storefront in a new city. The new site, or virtual storefront, will increase your consumer base and help establish your label's reputation as being solid and for real. If your product is everywhere, then you must be all right. Although some sites pay higher premiums than others, you'll adjust your expectations and distribute to most of them anyway. For example, eMusic pays a terrible premium that changes from quarter to quarter and generally floats around $.30 per download. Obviously iTunes's robust $.70 makes eMusic look like a joke. However, eMusic has a huge college-age audience that uses eMusic on a subscription basis. For you, this means consistent sales every month, no matter what. The subscription purchase formula appeals to one type of buyer, and eMusic lets you reach that different type of digital music consumer.

I used to have a weekly routine of going to the same three record stores on Tuesdays to pick up the new releases of the week. I started with my favorite record store, then worked my way down my chain of favorites if the first store didn't have what I wanted. Your fans still do this—only they do it digitally. Fans will prefer one site over another for a host of reasons that you can't influence. They get comfortable and keep returning. Since you understand this, you place your releases on several sites. You cast a wider net. You catch more fish.

13

How to Open Doors
(Without Breaking Them Down)

*I*n any business or mode of life—not just in the music industry—when you start out, no one will care about you. It's really okay. You have to start somewhere, and at the bottom is the likely place to begin. You just have to deal with that. But what you don't want is to end up staying at the bottom. You've got to climb up the ladder, as in every other business. But in the music industry there is a different set of rules.

Your goal is to position yourself in a way that makes you happy, but you'd like to do so without being obtrusive, annoying, disrespectful, or anything else that might damage your reputation and your chances for further success.

There are people in the music industry who have been there a very long time, and you must respect their seniority. You may want to do things differently than someone who has been working in the industry for twenty or thirty years, but you should never presume to know more than they do. There's a good reason for that: you don't. I don't care how hip or how smart you are, you will have to pay your dues, learn the ropes, look around the room and see how things are done before you clomp in there. I don't mean you should let folks walk all over you, but you can find a balance between eager input and overzealous enthusiasm. In short, you can be a pro.

How to get yourself through that front door can be daunting and frustrating. Even if your music is amazing, you still need key people—reviewers, writers, bloggers, booking agents—to take notice of it for that music to get out and into the world. It is your job to get your music noticed by those important people—and you're not the only one out there trying to do just that.

When attempting to make contact with a world in which I (as yet) have no reputation or connections, I've found that it's best to be honest and direct and let the music speak for itself.

Here's how I do it:

Hey there. My name is Ian Anderson and I run Afternoon Records. I'm new to the industry—but the music I represent is the best thing indie rock has seen since Foghat.

Here's an MP3 of our latest release. Let me know what you think. I have a hunch that you'll really enjoy it.

Thank you for your time,

Ian

Chances are an e-mail, phone call, or Morse code signal like this—or however you send your message—will be ignored. The folks you're contacting get lots of messages like this. You can make yours stand out by repeating your attempts, over and over; even if they don't return your calls, they might start to recognize your voice! And, even if they don't phone you back, that doesn't mean they aren't listening to the music. Keep chipping away. Chip, chip, chip.

Don't get discouraged. This doesn't mean you aren't valuable as a musical institution, it just means that your value is unknown at present. Once your value is known, then this process will become much easier and you can forget ever reading this chapter.

Right now, it is crucial that you stay persistent. Now, notice that I said *persistent* and not *annoying*. How not to be annoying is a fine line to walk. Don't send more than one e-mail a day about the same subject to the same person. If you really want Pitchfork to write back to you about the new Readers record, ask only once every few days, not five times every single day. Although you may want to do that, resist!

You also don't need to totally suck up. You are contacting someone who is important and busy, but he or she is just a person like you. Politeness is good; cheap flattery can feel phony. It does us little good to grovel at anyone's feet.

Convincing someone to take a chance on new music can be hard, but remember this: these folks really love music too. Just as we do. It's a thrill for them to find a great new sound. Just as it is for us. We have something in common with them, and we can build on that to create relationships. If your first few releases get ignored, that's just the way the cookie crumbles. You cannot get disheartened, and you must continue submitting the music you represent for review—don't stop sending, because if you stop sending your records, no one will ever review them, listen to them, buy them—or care about them.

14

Booking

I've never been one for sitting still and waiting for success to come to me. That is just not the way things work in the real world. Same for bands. Success won't come to your band while they lounge at the local coffee shop. They have to hit the road. When it comes to making a band break, touring is the best thing a band can do to grow a fan base and garner some cross-country reviews and audiences.

I love to tour, but not every musician does. It is often very difficult to coax a band to get into a van and start driving. I don't know why (because, as I said, I love to tour), but in my time running a label, I've found that most of the bands I have worked with just don't like to tour, because, well, touring is tough. Long drives, late nights, early mornings, no money, no food, high gas prices, and missing home—all pose huge obstacles. Somehow you must help your bands to overcome these obstacles and encourage them to tour, because touring leads to record sales and merch sales and revenue and fame and fortune and stardom and a spot on MTV.

The increased exposure that results from playing in a different city every night is beneficial in both visible and invisible ways. Just the mere fact that a band is touring is helpful. It indicates a level of seriousness and commitment that implies quality. If the show is on the road, it must be good. Furthermore, the more people a band plays in front of, the greater the likelihood that albums will be sold, connections will be fostered, and fans will be made. Do whatever it takes to get bands out of town, because it can only help them and you (the more bands on your label are touring, the more chances there will be to find out about your label). It may take tour-support funding, gas money, or even you going along with them—but do what it takes.

Once your band is ready to tour, you need bookings to tour to. The basic principles of logistics and coordination are generally the same, venue to venue, city to city, and state to state. That means you can sit down at the keyboard and telephone and book a tour just about anywhere in the country using the same methods.

Start with a database of clubs all over the country. If you don't have one, you have to make one. The best way to do this is take a look at like-minded bands' tour schedules. Bands that you think would play similar venues as the band you are pushing will help because you can glean their venue information very easily. Run down their list of tour dates and start doing research. Nearly every venue in America has a website or MySpace page with contact information for booking. It takes time to find the details, but it's worth the effort.

You can also get your band's feet wet for touring by booking a few local shows for starters. Local is a little easier because you don't need to do much research to find out where the clubs are and what their musical tastes are—you're local too. You know.

I've had good success with this approach. I let a venue know the likely age range of the audience and how many people the band tends to draw (you may have to estimate here), and I offer them a choice of dates. Don't give them too many dates; keep it under five ideal dates. If the venue e-mails or phones you to negotiate another date, that's great—consider it networking and a bit of conversation to cement a good working relationship.

Dear Venue We Love,

I have four bands ready to play with an all-ages draw of roughly 80 people and am looking for June 6, 7, 13, or 14. Do you have any of these dates open? If so, let's book it!

Let me know what you think,

Ian

Until a few years ago, the best way to book a show at any venue in the country was to submit a press kit to the venue months in advance of the date you wanted and follow up with the venue's booking agent a few weeks later. The process was much like submitting a record for review to a magazine or periodical. This is still a helpful thing to do from the club owner's perspective, and I recommend it. However, things are shifting a bit here, thanks to the ease of accessing bands' MySpace pages and electronic presskits (EPK). You can now send an easy e-mail to a booker (the person in charge of hiring acts for a venue) with a link to your MySpace page or EPK, to save yourself the postage and save the booker some room on his or her desk. Experiment. Try both.

The first two or three tours you book will be constant uphill battles (to get a response, to get a booker to answer the phone, to get a clear confirmation that you've got a date), but after bookers start to know who you are and what you have to offer, the process will grow easier.

Agents and bookers constantly receive submissions just like yours. Following the same philosophy you use when approaching a writer or editor, when you approach a booker, you need to make things easy, professional, and fast. While, of course, always conveying the fact that the band you are booking is great and deserves their attention. Here is a sample:

Dear Out-of-Town Venue in New York,

I have the Readers (Thankyou Records) routed through New York in July and we're looking for either the 14th, 15th, or 16th—do you have any openings?

Key points:
- *Charted #71 on the CMJ Top 200 last week*
- *KEXP Band of the Week earlier this month*
- *Tons of family in New York*

For more information, please visit myspace.com/thereaders band.

Let me know what you think,

Ian

A booking pitch can go ignored for weeks, so it is crucial to start the booking process early—at least three months before the dates that you want.

If the main venues in a given market are unable to host your band, you must explore every other venue option you can: houses, practice spaces, VFW halls, coffeeshops, record stores. Cast a wide net when booking a tour. Don't rely on one venue to come through. Ask every venue you know of in the same city for the same date. Hopefully, at least one is bound to bite. If one doesn't, move on to another city.

Once you have lassoed a date with a venue, it is imperative that you iron out the details in advance. Your band will be touring without you. You don't want your band to show up to the venue expecting one thing, the venue expecting another, and you being a thousand miles away. Some venues will send booking contracts for touring acts. However, many do not, and will expect you and your band to take them at their word—and expect the band to be flexible with last-minute changes as late as half an hour before the show. It helps to put everything in writing, and it's easy to do. After the details are hammered out, put them into an e-mail and send it to the booker and the band and keep one for yourself.

Details to iron out with the booker include the audience age restriction (if any), door price, start time, load-in time, preticketing outlet, hospitality, and door split. The band needs to know the load-in time, when they need to arrive and where, what hospitality will be provided (this may range anywhere from dinner to free drinks), and the door split. A door split is money that a band is paid based on a percentage taken from what the venue has made that night from people coming in the door. The door split needs to be worked out well ahead of time so that there aren't any miscommunications between the venue and the band.

Typically, the venue takes anywhere from 30 to 50 percent of the money brought in from the door. It's a good idea to get that percentage clearly spelled out and agreed upon so there isn't any confusion at the end of the night when it's time for the band to leave.

The next key element to line up is local support—in other words, other local bands to open for the band you're booking. One of the great things about being on tour is meeting people. In fact, that might in the end be the true goal of touring. I used to think touring was just to play for people, which ideally I think it is, but on a small level, it may in truth be more about networking and making friends. Part of that is not only meeting people who like the band, but also having the band meet other likeminded bands.

Encourage your band to be friendly with other bands they meet in each venue. You want them to build their own networks too. Here's why: if they make friends with other bands, then you can start instituting the glorious concept of the "show trade." This means that if Band X books your band with them in their hometown, you'll book Band X with your band in your hometown. Having a local band opening a show helps get people out to the show in the first place. If you're sending a small band out, they will attract a small crowd—if they have a crowd at all. When your band plays with local bands that gel well with your band, other bands' fans may take to liking your band too.

On top of that, venues like to see labels that are invested enough in their bands to take the time to set up a good bill with strong local support—not to mention that such a bill means more people through the door and into the club.

Booking is a touchy process. There is an extraordinarily fine line between a confirmation and a hold, and it is often more difficult to get a date at all when promoting bands and a label with little or no national clout or reputation.

As you spend more and more time developing and expanding your booking network, you will evolve greater subtleties in your approach, but the pointers above will get you through the door.

15

Marketing Plans

A marketing plan is a basic tool that keeps artists and labels and everyone else involved in promoting a record on the same page. Although drawing up a plan is a detailed task, you'll be glad to have it around. You should get into the routine of doing this for each release.

Here is the marketing plan Afternoon Records used for Haley Bonar's *Big Star* release. It is a straightforward example of how to formally set deadlines and spell out everyone's respective jobs.

HALEY BONAR—*Big Star*

PRODUCT OBJECTIVE
To expand on Haley's audience, to get radio play, to obtain synch licenses, to build her live audience.

STATEMENT
Haley Bonar is a Minnesota-based singer-songwriter who has made an incredibly accessible record. To say that it is her best record is selling it short. This is a fantastic record. Combine that with Haley's adorable looks, touring, and music that fits well to picture and the possibilities are vast.

Details

Album Title: *Big Star*
Producers: Tchad Blake, Haley Bonar
Album Selection Number: AR044
Album Street Date: 06/10/08
Musicians: Haley Bonar (vocals, guitar, Rhodes)
            Chris Morrissey (bass)
            Dave King (drums)
Label: Afternoon Records
Management Contact: Andrea Troolin—Ekonomisk Management
            email@heraddress.com
Booking Agent: Paul Gillis—Ripple Entertainment, LLC
            email@hisaddress.com
Publishing: Spit Comet Music (BMI)
Publicity/Marketing /A&R: Afternoon Records
            ian@afternoonrecords.com
            Ian Anderson
Track Listing: 1. Green Eyed Boy
                    2. Arms a Harm
                    3. Little Maiden Gin
                    4. Big Star
                    5. May Day
                    6. Better Half
                    7. Something Great
                    8. Queen of Everything
                    9. Highway 16
                   10. Along
                   11. Tiger Boy

College Radio

Big Star is Haley's most accessible record to date, especially for radio. We expect that we will have solid college radio support but will aim to build far beyond that into noncommercial/NPR and commercial AAA [adult album alternative] support. This album is tailor-made for AAA radio. Internet/satellite radio will also be serviced.

We will endeavor to get radio support/radio visits along tour dates. Live performances will be pitched to *World Café*, *Morning Becomes Eclectic*, *Mountain Stage*, *CityFolk*, *E-Town*, etc.

Charting History: #6 CMJ ADD, #2 AAA ADD, #68 CMJ Top 200

05/21—400 copies of *Big Star* and 400 one-sheets are delivered to Vitriol Independent Promotions

05/23—Vitriol ships to 400 college radio stations, noncommercial AAA, and specialty radio

06/03—*Big Star* goes for Adds and AAA

Haley is confirmed to do on-air performance and Song of the Day download feature on Minneapolis's 89.3 *The Current* the week of release and will also be doing sessions with KTCZ and KUOM after the record release show.

We will also target tastemakers—Kevin Cole @ KEXP, Bruce Warren @ WXPN, Rita Houston @ WFUV, Chris Douridas @ KCRW, etc., for early VIP packages.

NPR—local and all national programmers—Bob Boilen, *All Things Considered*, etc.

Suggested Singles: Release date: "Something Great"—June 10, 2008
Estimated release date: "Big Star"—November 2008
Estimated release date: "Green Eyed Boy"—April 2008

Target Market: 18–25 college-aged and 25–40 AAA listeners
Sales Forecast: 5,000 units within 6 months
                Initial shipment is 3,000 units
Suggested Retail Price: $12.99

TARGETED MEDIA

We'll work to raise Haley's profile in music and entertainment magazines / online outlets as a talented musician / songwriter / "star on the rise" while trying to extend her reputation as not just a Minneapolis/ Midwestern artist but to build a NATIONAL PROFILE.

Music and Entertainment Media
    Major National /Lifestyle Outlets, Print:

Spin	*The Big Takeover*
Billboard	*AMP Magazine*
Revolver	*Skyscraper*
Magnet	*Bust*
Venus	*Entertainment Weekly*
Paste	*The New Yorker*
Blender	*Rolling Stone*
CMJ	*People*
Performing Songwriter	*Men's Journal*
Paper	*The Wall Street Journal*
Esquire	*USA Today*
The New York Times	*Newsweek*
Time	*Vanity Fair*
Details	*GQ*
Elle	*Interview*
Vogue	*Wired*
Alternative Press	*Utne Reader*

Major Dailies / Key Regionals, with particular focus on L.A., N.Y., San Francisco, Chicago, D.C., Boston, Seattle, Portland, Nashville, San Diego, Austin, Minneapolis

Television—Pitch her to Jim Pitt for Conan O'Brien, Sheila @ Letterman, Oprah Winfrey, *Late Late Show*, Minneapolis TV outlets, MTV 52/52

Online—focused attention to blogs, social-networking sites, YouTube, AOL Spinner, PitchforkTV

Stream the album one month out on Afternoon's or Haley's website.

Pick one song for free MP3 download one week before release.

Video—Ali Selim (*Sweet Land*) will direct a video in June.

Publicity effort led by Ian Anderson

Full-service CD ships to mailing list of 250 on 5.15.08

Early confirmations already from: *Star Tribune, City Pages, Pioneer Press, Minnesota Monthly Magazine, Mpls/St. Paul Magazine*

LICENSING
Zync Music to represent Haley's music for synchronization opportunities. They are confident there is great potential for the album in this arena and will be aggressive with pitching her music in this realm.

Fox TV Music	NBC Universal Television Music
New Line Cinema	Chop Shop Music Supervision
Little Mountain	Sony Pictures Entertainment
Gavin & Gavin	Warner Bros. TV Music

BLOGS

Pitchfork Media	Brooklyn Vegan
My Old Kentucky Blog	Stereogum
Gorilla vs. Bear	You Ain't No Picasso
More Cowbell	Music for Robots
Rock Sellout	The Music Slut
Over 100 others	

RETAIL

Overview: Haley has made fans at retail with her last two records, *The Size of Planets*, which has soundscanned 3,200, and *Lure the Fox*, which has sold approximately 2,700.

She is firmly established in Minneapolis; we hope to build from this a larger national sales base.

Account Activity

Local:

Cheapo	Endcaps/Listening Stations
Electric Fetus	New Releases/Listening Stations

National Retailers:

Borders	Borders Free Download on Borders.com
Best Buy	Focus markets in Midwest
Barnes and Noble	Endcaps/Listening Stations
Target	Red Room Endcap—only if it is worth it!
CIMS	AIMS

Waterloo Records Listening Stations

240 Retailers will receive press kits and posters direct from Afternoon Records encouraging the store to order the record through Koch.

Two Album Posters (1,000 each) to be made and shipped to retailers and venues.

Afternoon Records street teams to distribute posters to indie record stores.

Digital Retail

Big Star will be sold on over 80 digital retailers. Namely and most focused on: iTunes, eMusic, SnoCap, Amazon, Rhapsody.

Internet Marketing

Blogs, Facebook, MySpace, Buzznet

Tour Support

As-needed basis, I want HB on tour so I'll do what it takes.

Timeline

May 12—Press, Initial Mailing
        Subsequent and Specialty Mailings Weekly Hereafter
May 12—Blogs, Initial Mailing
        Blog MP3 Single Schedule:
           Release date: "Something Great"—June 10, 2008
           Estimated release date: "Big Star"—July 14, 2008
           Estimated release date: "Green Eyed Boy"—August 25, 2008
June 3—College radio ADD Date
June 3—AAA/specialty radio ADD Date
June 3 to 27—Major-market tour with Hayden
June 10—National street date
June 12—CD release party at the Varsity Theater
June 14—Haley to open for Amos Lee at the Minnesota Zoo
June and beyond—Tour support
Perpetual: campaigns begin 6 weeks prior to first tour date in a given leg.

16

Getting the Word Out

Publicity and promotion are vital for the growth of both your label and your bands. You have faith in them, you want to grow both them and your label, and promotion and publicity, done well, will get that job done (with a little luck added in). The first thing you need to do is build a clear and simple promotional package that piques the interest of distributors, press, radio stations, and clubs—anyone you want interested in you.

Basic Promotional Tools

It's time to create the one-sheet for the band. What is a one-sheet? I'm glad you asked. It is the universal constant in the world of music promotion. It's simply an $8\frac{1}{2}$" x 11" piece of paper; on it, you print a photo of the band plus information about the band and its music.

Sit behind the desk of a music writer or a radio station programming director for a make-believe moment. What would you rather get in the mail?

a. A solitary CD in an envelope without any sort of description or explanation.
b. A not-so-solitary CD in an envelope along with an $8\frac{1}{2}$" x 11" sheet of paper with a photo, band bio, quotes from past reviews, and contact info for the label and the artist.

The correct answer is: b.

This is what needs (at least) to be on your one-sheet:

- Artist name (on the top, really big)
- Title of the album (big, but not bigger than the band name)
- A high-resolution (300 dpi) promo photo of the band (300 dpi means 300 dots per inch, which indicates the resolution of the photo. In order to prevent your photo from looking blurry, blotchy, or pixelated, you will want to make sure that every photo is hi-res so that everything you release looks good.)
- Picture of the CD cover (hi-res, 300 dpi)
- A brief 100- to 200-word bio of the artist(s)
- Complete track listing with the important tracks emphasized in some way (bold, italicized, starred, etc.)
- Key quotes from other publications that look good and might grease the wheels (past reviews go here)
- Contact information (including phone, e-mail, website, MySpace page)
- Label logo

Since the band's one-sheet will be used in almost every type of promo and publicity you'll send out, spend a little time putting the pieces together properly. Spell-check. Lay it out nicely. Avoid that thrown-together-in-my-mom's-basement look.

Here are the one-sheets on my desk right now:

John Krueger (bass), Grace Fiddler (vocals, synth), Ian Anderson (vocals, guitar), Bill Caperton (guitar), Elliot Manthey (drums).

Minneapolis-natives **One for the Team** have found a new and happy home with Long Beach, California's the Militia Group, who will be releasing their sophomore album in August 2008. One for the Team made waves with their first album "Good Boys Don't Make Noise" (enclosed), finding themselves on the CMJ Top 200 charts for 14 weeks, playing over 100 tour dates across the country, and sharing the stage with the likes of Voxtrot, Someone Still Loves You Boris Yeltsin, Rooney, British Sea Power, Georgie James, Tapes 'n Tapes, Tilly and the Wall, Headlights, Page France and Aqueduct.

Now heading into their first release as a part of the Militia Group family, One for the Team has 180 tour dates planned, a new van, and really great haircuts.

One for the Team

"Few 21-year-olds in the biz work harder than Ian Anderson, founder of Afternoon Records."
- *SPIN Magazine (4.07)*

"A staggeringly great debut!" - "Excellent." - "Wunderkind." - "Picked to Click 2006" - "One of the Top Albums of 2006" - "Best New Bands of 2006"
- *Pulse of the Twin Cities, Pioneer Press, Star Tribune, City Pages, RadioK (Fall and Winter 2006)*

"Meet 21-year-old Ian Anderson, a Minneapolis college student, record-label head, and brainchild for this squeaky-clean indie-rock outfit - not quite as riffy as Built to Spill, but probably just fine for Death Cab cuties." - *The Village Voice (8.06)*

"Ian Anderson has a voice that could melt any girl's heart." – *Howewastheshow.com (6.06)*

"One For the Team has stolen my heart, alas." - *Stage Hymns (7.06)*

"Power pop for the people, modern day bubblegum with razor-sharp hooks."
- *Bands to Watch 2008, Metro Magazine (1.08)*

THE MILITIA GROUP   Label Contact:

Band Contact:
Ian Anderson
onefortheteammusic@gmail.com
ian@afternoonrecords.com

HALEY BONAR
BIG STAR

Haley Bonar is twenty-four years old and already on her fourth album. Her new album, *Big Star*, is a watershed moment for her: simple on the intake, but reveals universal truths with a powerful emotional impact as it sinks in. In the words of filmmaker Ali Selim (Sweet Land) "Her voice is an invitation to amazing places."

Big Star is Bonar's new and most accomplished collection of songs, an album loosely themed around the struggle of wanting something that elicits both dislike and desire – whether it be fame, success, or love. The album was recorded at the Terrarium in Minneapolis and mixed by noted engineer Tchad Blake (Tom Waits, The Bad Plus, Elvis Costello, Pearl Jam) who brings all of the subtle textures of the recordings to life. Haley played guitars, melotron and keyboards, and was joined by Chris Morrissey (Ben Kweller) on bass, Dave King (The Bad Plus) on drums, and Luke Anderson and Bill Mike on electric guitar. The album will be released June 3, 2008 on Afternoon Records.

Won "Best American Roots Artist" and *Lure the Fox* won "Best American Roots Recording" in the 2006 Minnesota Music Awards and nominated for best female vocalist.

"Artists of the Year" – *City Pages (12.06)*

"Best Albums of 2006" – *Star Tribune, City Pages, Pulse, The Onion (12.06)*

Best Song of 2006 ("Us") – *Pulse of the Twin Cities (12.06)*

SPIN Artist of the Day (11.30.06)

Lasso'd by Daytrotter in April 2007

Out June 10th on Afternoon Records

Afternoon Records
mpls, mn.
www.afternoonrecords.com

Publicity and Label:
Ian Anderson
ian@afternoonrecords.com

Management:
Andrea Troolin
andrea@ekonomiskmgmt.com

DREW DANBURRY

Drew Danburry is a musician who has toured independently and released records independently for approximately five years or so. He can't remember all the specifics of his wack life; otherwise we'd know all the embarrassing details. We know that he grew up in Southern California and in high school he released a cassette tape of Eazy-E inspired gangster rap tunes recorded with keyboard and an organ. He was notoriously known as "White Chocolate" and his cassette release of "4-eva" still remains to be found, along with several of his many other free styling sessions and mix tapes that at some point unabashedly circled the underground hip hop scene like wildfire. Drew maintains that they were not good, or even laughable.

Since those hazy days of his youth, Drew has relocated to Utah and pumped out jams with friends under bands of various names, including the The Danburrys, who recorded together but disbanded before they could go out on tour. So Drew did it on his own.

While selling homemade copies of his first album "An Introduction To Sex Rock", he began touring with just his guitar in a little red car. In 2005 he re-released his first album "An Introduction To Sex Rock" and a second album "Besides: Are We Just Playing Around Out Here Or Do We Mean What We Say?" and began touring nationally with bands like Lydia, The Robot Ate Me and Aubrey Debauchery.

2006 brought about a seven-month national tour, where Drew tried to play anywhere and everywhere people would let him. There were short stints with Harry and the Potters, Aubrey Debauchery, TaughtMe and Seve vs. Evan. This experience allowed Drew to book a European tour, which also led to his 2007 release, Drew Danburry/Fatal Fury and the Lasercats' "Live In France" recorded at two separate shows while he was overseas. In July 2007 Drew marked his 500th show at Kilby Court in Salt Lake City since his tour kickoff there in February 2005, and decided to take a break.

But not for long.

2008 has marked the release of the Mother EP, a resurgence in his touring schedule, and his forthcoming full length, "This Could Mean Trouble, You Don't Speak for the Club", out November 4, 2008 on Emergency Umbrella Records.

With wit, wondrously catchy hits, and a beard that reflects the length of time he's been on the road, it's about time to see what Drew Danburry is all about.

VITRIOL

Publicity Contact:

Ian Anderson
Ian@vitriolpromotion.com
www.vitriolpromotion.com

Alyssa Kleven

www.vitriolpromotion.com

NOW, NOW EVERY CHILDREN

DEBUT FULL-LENGTH **CARS** AVAILABLE ONLINE 11.08.09 & IN STORES 12.09.08

"CACIE'S INNOCENTLY EARNEST VOICE STEALS THE SHOW, WHILE THE MUSIC SWIRLS AROUND HER, MANAGING TO PUSH HER HIGHER STILL."

– 3HIVE

1. CACIE DALAGER / VOCALS, GUITAR, KEYS
2. BRADLEY HALE / DRUMS, VOCALS

Don't let their name fool you. Now, Now Every Children might be kind of short, and kind of adorable, but their music is of the larger-than-life variety.

Back before Now, Now Every Children was just a name, then-children Cacie Dalager (vocals, guitar) and Brad Hale (drums) started writing songs together after marching band practice in Blaine, Minn. Their first work of art well-wished a graduating friend from high school, but their musical queues were much more than greeting card salutations. Dalager and Hale began recording demos in their suburban basements, posting them on MySpace and gaining fans before they even played a show.

After signing to Afternoon Records in 2007, Now, Now Every Children released two EPs to critical acclaim: "Not One, But Two" and "In the City." Their lo-fi recordings in combina-

tion with Dalager's heartbreaking voice championed the attention of some of the harshest critics of all, their peers, earning a spot as "Band of the Month" on Paramorefans.com.

"Cars," Now, Now Every Children's first full-length album is all about life on the highway. Rerecording 3 of the singles off their first two EPs plus 7 more brand new tracks "Cars" is a series of poignant moments written by Dalager and Hale, mostly over the last year. Since then they've ventured outside their Midwestern routes and played a select west coast tour, as well as shared the stage with Mates of State, the Rosebuds, Say Hi and Cloud Cult.

CARS

BAND OF THE DAY / THE DAILY CHORUS 02.20.08
BAND OF THE MONTH / PARAMOREFANS.COM 03.08

LABEL / MGMT / BOOKING
IAN@AFTERNOONRECORDS.COM

WWW.AFTERNOONRECORDS.COM
MYSPACE.COM/NOWNOWEVERYCHILDREN

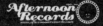

Afternoon Records

You might argue that the layouts for Afternoon Records' artists are almost too simple. But that's our style. I think there shouldn't be excessive distractions and that one-sheets should make it easy for writers and booking agents to find what they need to know.

But your new label can play by its own one-sheet rules. The one-sheets from Vitriol have a grittier approach. You might take that spin with Thankyou Records. You aren't locked in to only one one-sheet approach, of course. In fact, I recommend that you remodel your one-sheets a few times per year, or even with each new one-sheet.

Electronic Press Kit (EPK)

I hate the term *electronic press kit*. It just sounds lame. But the thing itself is not. An EPK is an interactive version of a band's one-sheet. It's placed online, often on a social networking site, such as MySpace. Everything about a band is there: a few MP3s to play, a brief bio, some links to dates and venues for upcoming shows, contact info, etc.

That MySpace page is essential, but still, you can't rely solely on MySpace to do your promoting and showcasing for you. You need to push a little harder than that and build an entirely separate, self-supported site where you can control the content and appearance of your EPK.

A well-designed and well-thought-out EPK offers members of the press one-stop shopping for all the info they need to write a killer review of your release. And if they want an interview, the EPK steers them toward your press contact (probably you).

An effective EPK contains all the information on the one-sheet but with a few extra bells and whistles.

Lead off with a header of the band's name and then a nice promo photo below it, just like a one-sheet. But now, before digging in and giving the reader the band's bio and tons of information about them, provide the opportunity for the reader to discover this new world for themselves. Post links to press materials, the band's MySpace page, two or three downloadable MP3s, a few key press quotes, two or three upcoming shows, and then the illustrious bio.

Below is a rough template for one possible EPK design. I like to keep it simple and easy. The coolest thing about an EPK is that it offers the reader options. Instead of just one promo photo, you can post three or four, for example—or even a video link.

Under the "Press Materials" section, you can post links for downloading a PDF version of the one-sheet you have worked so hard to make, three or four additional hi-res photos, and also a hi-res version of a band's album cover. Providing the cover is critical—don't skimp here. Ever wonder what makes an arts editor print a photo of one band but not another? Having a high-resolution, high-quality, interesting photo at the ready at 1:00 a.m., that's what. A big part of getting good publicity is delivering good raw materials to writers and editors, to make it as easy as possible for them to cover your bands.

Under the "Downloads" section, a reader can click a button and listen to the band while sinking their teeth into the nitty-gritty of the band's inner workings and backstory. Here, you should post at least one of the band's singles. I've seen a few EPKs that actually provide the entire album for streaming or a zip file of the entire album for download. Both of these are viable options. However, I recommend streaming because you don't want to be giving away the album—you want to sell it!

Here's an example of an EPK that could be used for One for the Team:

BANDS///**ONE FOR THE TEAM**

Grace Fiddler (vocals, synth), Ian Anderson (vocals, guitar), Elliot Manthey (drums)

Listen:
  MySpace Page
Press Materials:
  Press one-sheet (PDF)
  Hi-res promo photo (1)
  Hi-res promo photo (2)
  Hi-res promo photo (3)
  Hi-res promo photo (4)
  Build It Up hi-res album cover (PDF)
Booking:
  booking@afternoonrecords.com
Press:
  ian@vitriolpromotion.com
Downloads:
  "Apples" off of *Build It Up* (click to download)
  "Build It Up" off of *Build It Up* (click to download)

"I Promised I'd Grow Up" off of *Good Boys Don't Make Noise*
(click to download)

Bio:

One for the Team is an American indie-rock band based out of Minneapolis, Minnesota. Founded by the American songwriter Ian Anderson, twenty-four, in 2006, the band has released two full-length albums, *Good Boys Don't Make Noise* in 2006 on Afternoon Records and *Build It Up* in 2008 on the Militia Group and Afternoon Records, and one EP, *Build a Garden*, in 2009. The band is completed by the co-lead-vocalist and keyboard player Grace Fiddler, twenty, and the drummer Elliot Manthey, twenty-two.

History:

Originally intended as an outlet for Anderson's pop songs that didn't quite fit the aesthetic of his first band, Aneuretical, One for the Team started as a strictly studio side project with Manthey and John Krueger, the band's original bass player. In 2006, One for the Team released *Good Boys Don't Make Noise* on Anderson's own Afternoon Records and received a mass of critical acclaim, which moved the project from the studio and onto the stage.

Although receiving attention almost exclusively via blogs and building large fanbases in New York, Los Angeles, Britain, Germany, and Japan, One for the Team stuck to the Midwest while Anderson finished his undergraduate degree in English at Saint Olaf College in Northfield, Minnesota.

After several tours, multiple member changes, which included Bill Caperton of Ela, One for the Team settled on its current lineup, which features Fiddler, Manthey, and the bass player Jacob Huelster, formerly of Look Down.

The addition of Fiddler was integral to what is now considered the band's sound: dual vocals. Anderson and Fiddler share vocal duties almost equally as the pair sing in unison throughout their most recent albums and during live shows.

***Build It Up*:**

One for the Team's sophomore album, *Build It Up*, was recorded in

Minneapolis, Minnesota, in April 2008 at Fur Seal Studios with Rob Skoro and Joe Johnson. Released jointly by the Militia Group and Afternoon Records on August 19, 2008, the album received critical acclaim and was featured by *Spin*, NPR, and MTV, and the band recorded a Daytrotter Session in Rock Island, Illinois, in December 2008. The band toured extensively after the release, visiting thirty-eight states and playing more than 180 tour dates and spent time on the road with Dressy Bessy, Frightened Rabbit, the French Kicks, So Many Dynamos, Someone Still Loves You Boris Yeltsin, and Select Start.

Build a Garden:

One for the Team's third album, *Build a Garden*, is an eight-song EP that was recorded by One for the Team in their apartment in Minneapolis and released by Afternoon Records. It was engineered, mixed, and produced by Anderson entirely in his bedroom. Released on April 14, 2009, the EP is composed of four songs from *Build It Up* rearranged and rerecorded, and four new songs. There was a limited pressing of five hundred hand-made copies and it is available for digital download.

Discography:

Good Boys Don't Make Noise (2006; Afternoon Records)

Build It Up (2008; The Militia Group / Afternoon Records)

Build a Garden EP (2009; Afternoon Records)

Band Members:

Ian Anderson: Vocals and Guitar

Grace Fiddler: Vocals and Keyboard

Elliot Manthey: Drums

Jacob Huelster: Bass

Past Members:

John Krueger: Bass (2006–2008)

Bill Caperton: Guitar (2007–2008)

Bryan Sonday: Guitar (2006–2007)

Sam Gerard: Keyboards (2006–2007)

Brett Bullion: Drums (2006)

Free Stuff

Other than these basics, when sending out a record, remember that people love to get free stuff. At Thankyou Records, you won't have a whole lot of disposable income to spend on things you'll just give away. But you are innovative and imaginative and you look for opportunities. So if you've got enough bucks to print up stickers, posters, buttons, pens, coasters, whatever, give it a try. Anything that sets your bands apart. Anything that starts a little buzz.

17

Radio Promotion

Radio promotion is the most basic and uniform way to market your release. Most everyone listens to the radio: either intentionally in the car, scrambling between stations to find something agreeable to kill some rush hour time; or passively, while shopping for groceries, renting a movie, or buying that new Prada backpack.

You may feel the deck is stacked against you in radio. We've all heard stories about "payola" schemes in which DJs and radio companies are "incentivized" to play certain records—the incentives being anything from money to favors to freebies. And yes, Clear Channel owns a gazillion stations where programs are set by people you and I can't get to.

And sure, we all hear the same five bands ripping off Nirvana on the nationally syndicated, yet locally broadcast, Alternative Top 40 radio stations—you know, the ones with that really annoying "Let's rawk!" guy who spins Soundgarden as if he had just discovered them earlier that week.

College Radio

But what I am talking about is college radio: the noncommercial and pretty-darn-close-to-pure-and-honest radio universe. *Now Ian*, you may be thinking, *What possible influence could college radio have over the future of my release?* Everything. The college market serves as the barometer for what is *actually* interesting and what is *actually* going on in the national music scene. Let me explain.

The reason college radio is such a great way to determine interest and popularity is because everything college stations broadcast is chosen, not paid for. College radio stations don't receive checks in the mail or get bribes. There are no games to play. College stations play records that their DJs like, their friends like, and probably what most eighteen- to twenty-two-year-olds like, because they are all eighteen- to twenty-two-year-old music fans who are involved in radio and the promotion of music for the love of it. And that's why it is so crucial to get in with this crowd.

If you ever want to achieve "overnight" success, this is one of the best ways to do it. You can either run your promotion campaign through a company, or you can do it yourself and/or start your own radio promotions company. Your success will have a lot to do with name recognition: if there is a trusted name on the return address label (which is why you might do this through a company if you're just starting), radio stations will open your mailed-in promotional copy of a CD first. If they've never heard of you, your disc may go to the bottom of the pile.

The objective of running a national radio campaign is threefold. First, some four hundred stations may start playing your stuff and four hundred music directors have heard of you. Promotional copies of your album are sent out to four hundred college and specialty radio stations across the country, along with one-sheets and stickers indicating recommended tracks for quick listening. Suddenly, overnight, at least four hundred people all over the country now know about your band. Not bad. Not to mention that those four hundred people are music directors at radio stations and, chances are, they like to talk about the music they like. If they like your music, that's a good thing.

Second, you'll get fans on college campuses nationwide. Your release will, hopefully, be played on at least some of those radio stations, catch some listeners' ears, and win over a fan or two, resulting in a few going to a show and perhaps buying an album or a T-shirt.

Third, you'll climb onto the CMJ Top 200 charts. *CMJ* stands for the *College Music Journal*, which many in the industry consider one of the best barometers for "what's next" in the independent music world. If you place on the Top 200, your record is one of the top two hundred most frequently spun records on college radio stations in the nation. As a result, people will pay attention. The more frequently your releases are played, the higher you climb up the charts. The higher you climb on the charts, the more waves your release makes. The more waves your release makes, the more people start to notice and maybe, just maybe, go out and buy your records from one of the stores in your already excellent distribution network.

Every college radio station is assigned a value between one and six that corresponds to its size in relation to all other college stations in the country and represents that station's "weight." For instance, KSTO (the St. Olaf College station in Northfield, Minnesota) has a weight of one, while KCMP (MPR's *The Current* in the Twin Cities) and KEXP (Seattle's huge and awesome station) each have a weight of six—the weightiest a station can get. The bigger the station, the higher the weight; the higher the weight, the greater the influence the station has. You want to get your records played on the biggest stations you can, because that will help push your records higher on the charts and reach a greater number of people per spin.

Every week, each college station reports to the CMJ their Top 30 chart of their most frequently played records. Each slot on this Top 30 has a value. A number-one chart position is assigned a value of thirty points, while a number-thirty chart position is assigned a value of one point. The point value corresponding to the chart position of a record is then multiplied by the weight of the station. That total is added to the totals from all the other stations that are charting the record. The more points you get, the higher you place on the charts, and so on. For instance, if a song charts at number one at a station with a weight of one, it is assigned 30 points. If that same record charts at number one at a station with a weight of five, it is assigned 150 points. Get it? Placing on the CMJ Top 200 is the one of the best ways for your label to build up a résumé. It says you've achieved enough critical success to go over well with the toughest of critics: college students. Plus, it shows that you have initiative.

You can run a campaign in-house or you can hire out. It's hard work: you package four hundred press kits, mail them out to the radio stations, and follow up *every* week asking if your CD is getting played. If it is, you thank them, and if it isn't, you try to persuade them to play it. If you hire out, full campaigns can cost anywhere from $1,200 to $3,000. If you do it yourself, invite friends over and order pizza.

If one of your Thankyou Records releases begins to do well and gets a positive response from certain schools, it's time to act. The first thing to do is to follow up with those stations that have fallen in love with your band and dish out a solid thank you, then expand on that opportunity. Ask if the stations' DJs would be interested in doing an interview with the band—over the phone or on the air, in person—or if they would be interested in having the band come and play on campus.

Beyond college radio is the growing—and, let's hope, by the time this book is published, soon-to-be-dominant world of subscription-based satellite radio companies, which currently means Sirius XM Radio, Inc.

You reach out to Sirius XM Radio in the same way you approach college radio. You submit your new release to them for review and approval, and if they like it, they'll play it. The beauty of satellite radio is that it offers so many channels aimed at very specific demographics of listeners that you can target your release to specific audiences. In addition, your release might be spun on any one of a large number of satellite stations—so one contact can work in many places. Satellite radio is a big winner in record stores, movie rental stores, and even hair salons, so it can hit a lot of passive listeners. Don't overlook it.

18

The Importance of Blogs
to an Independent Record Label

Blogs, blogs, blogs, blah, blah, blah. We hear so much about them, but why exactly are music blogs so awesome—and, more important, so essential to the survival of music labels? The very accurate answer is that music blogs are the new lifeblood of an independent record label; music blogs are the only surefire way to sell records and get to the audience that we're all trying so hard to reach.

From a consumer media standpoint, blogs are perfect. They are the purest form of opinion available today and therefore can be trusted by the loyal readership of the music blogosphere.

It has been my personal experience that more blog chatter results in more album sales. In 2007, Afternoon Records' biggest sellers were releases by Poison Control Center, We All Have Hooks for Hands, and Mouthful of Bees. Each record received a considerable amount of blog chatter. As of March 2008, Poison Control Center had received more than a hundred blog reviews; We All Have Hooks for Hands had received roughly seventy; and Mouthful of Bees had received sixty online and consumer media reviews. Each of these numbers accurately corresponds with album sales, putting Poison Control Center at the top, with Hooks and Bees close behind. In 2006, blogs were still a new element in the Afternoon Records promotional model, but the two biggest sellers from Afternoon Records in 2006 were One for the Team and Haley Bonar, who each received more blog chatter than any other release to date.

Releases that have not sold particularly well received little or no blog chatter. The influence of blogs is staggering. The difference between selling 25 records and 1,500 records often depends on the opinion of four or five bloggers—no joke. This is why blogs are so important.

A 2008 study of blog-chatter influence on album sales conducted by a group of NYU students showed the same results: "We analyzed the usefulness of blogs and social networks, as well as reviews in consumer, online media, and mainstream media, in predicting album sales in the four weeks before and after the album's release date. We found that the most significant variable is blog chatter or the volume of blog posts on an album, with higher numbers of posts corresponding to higher sales." This shows the absolute importance of including blogs in any successful publicity and promotional campaign. Reasons why?

The first, and perhaps the most important, reason is that those who read blogs are excited enough about new music to seek it out themselves. A consistent and loyal blog reader is always on the lookout for something new and exciting to get into. These are the people who go to record stores and buy albums, download records illegally over bit torrents, and download records legally through iTunes. They don't want to be force-fed music, they want to discover it for themselves through what they would consider proper channels, which may be more appropriately described as *personal* channels. These are the savvy people who are willing and able to go the extra mile to get a piece of music that they love. It's this sort of excitement that is contagious and inspiring and will be the spearhead of any sort of buzz building that you can put together.

The second reason why blogs matter is how easy blogs make it to purchase music. Usually every review includes a link or at least some clue about how to buy the music the writer is blogging about. Be it through iTunes, eMusic, or directly through the label, bloggers put in that extra effort so readers won't have to. If you connect the dots a little, a reader who stumbles upon a positive review of a band, listens to the MP3 provided, and likes it, is only two clicks away from owning the track. When it comes to reading something in a magazine or hearing a song on the radio, the reader or listener must follow up on their interest with a trip to the record store or a separate search of a digital music site. And that may or may not happen depending on the average consumer's attention span and interest level. That is the beauty of a blog. It's right there, right now. No extra effort required.

The 2008 study continued:

> Although we found that user-generated content is a good predictor of music album sales, our analysis showed that traditional factors cannot be ignored. While independent label releases with extremely high blog chatter can sell even more units than major label releases, our findings estimated that the average major label release sold approximately twelve times more than the average independent label release. We also found that the higher the number of mainstream media reviews, the greater the sales.
>
> The results of this study suggest that user-generated content should be considered seriously by record labels. Most notably, since blog chatter and MySpace friend information is available *before* an album releases and ships, record labels can examine these two variables to predict future sales well in advance of when the album is available in stores.

Thinking realistically, you may never be able to completely bridge the gap, but blogs can help you give the majors a run for their money.

19

Merchandising Deals

*I*t grows increasingly clear that music sales will never be as strong as they once were. Although the thing that you produce and promote is music, you cannot depend entirely upon music sales to sustain your label, because the album will very soon no longer be the staple product of the music business. The staple revenue source of the future may, sadly, be something along the lines of tour souvenirs. I say sadly, because I love music more than T-shirts. But as long as you recognize the writing on the wall and adjust your business plans accordingly, you can make the most of this trend.

You must seek different streams of revenue to help bridge the ever increasing gap between recording advances and CD sales revenue. The most obvious way? Merchandising: you slap your bands' names on T-shirts, buttons, stickers, tote bags, and pretty much anything you can think of. First you need to make these things, then you need to sell them online, at shows, or out of your trunk.

Before you invest in a run of a hundred four-color T-shirts or ten thousand buttons, you need to reach an agreement with each of your artists. This agreement can be included in your formal contracts or you can draft another contract (or attachment) to include as an "exhibit" of each contract. Since merchandising is such an important and specific area, I think the latter approach is more prudent.

The best way to do this is simply to design, manufacture, and distribute all merchandise bearing the moniker and likeness of your bands yourself, and to provide each band with a royalty for every sale.

When it comes to merchandise other than recordings, your profit margins will always be a bit thinner. With T-shirts, you should expect to pay anywhere from $5 to $9 per shirt, and you can't expect to charge any more than $10 to $15. Yes, we all see bands on tour charging $20 to $25 for shirts—and bigger bands might get away with that—but for your young label and your new bands, that is just too much.

The point is, you can nearly double your revenue if you can add the sale of a T-shirt to every album sale. Or you can sell a T-shirt live at a show, and that might spark the fan to go home and download an album.

Merchandising Contract

Here, with an explanation following each section, is a rough sketch of what your merchandising contract should look like:

1. We and any of our licensees shall have the exclusive right to use your legal and professional names, pictures, likenesses, and other identification of you ("Artist Indicia"), in connection with the manufacture, advertising, sales, and/or distribution of products and merchandise other than phonograph records as follows: (a) via mail order and retail outlets and (b) via an exclusive online store for the sale of such products and merchandise of your Artist Indicia (individually and collectively).

Thankyou Records has the exclusive right to use any sort of artwork or pictures of the band to sell any kind of merchandise you can justify making. This agreement has to do with everything that isn't a CD or any other audio product; this is dealing only with material products known as merchandise. And, as such, that merchandise is going to be sold through mail order, in some retail outlets, and online through your label's store.

2. Our right in and to merchandising shall be for a term that is coterminous with the term set by the Artist Agreement in regards to the recorded master hereof. After the termination of such term, we shall have an additional six (6) months within which to sell off any remaining inventory. If any inventory is remaining after such six-month period, then you shall exercise one of the following two options exercisable by written notice from you at any time after the end of such six-month period:

    a. Purchase all such inventory from us at our actual cost (including any and all shipping and handling costs and expenses).

    b. Require us to destroy all remaining inventory.

Thankyou Records will make and sell this merchandise for a term that coincides with the term named in the main recording contract. If the contract is signed for two records, you'll make merchandise and sell it for that same time period. If at any point that original contract is terminated, then Thankyou Records has six months to sell off and discontinue the line of merchandise regarding the artist. After those six months, the artist can elect to buy the remainder of the merchandise or ask you to destroy the inventory.

3. In full consideration for Merchandising Uses, we shall pay Artist a royalty of fifty percent (50%) of our net profits (otherwise known as net receipts after deduction of any out-of-pocket expenses, i.e., actual costs of origination, handling, and warehousing).

All the profit that Thankyou Records brings in will be split fifty-fifty with the artist. I think this is the best approach because it continues the spirit of the original arrangement in regard to album sales. Plus, it just seems to be the fairest solution.

4. No monies payable to you in connection with merchandising shall be utilized to offset any unrecouped advances or other monies which are recoupable by us or reimbursable by you to us for reasons not specifically pertaining to merchandising hereunder.

None of the income brought in by these endeavors will be counted toward recouping. This is nice because for both the label and the artist such income is just money that goes right into both pockets, rather than forcing the artist to dump another source of income into recouping.

5. Artist shall have the right to approve each design in consideration to be used for such merchandising.

Basically, this ensures that Thankyou Records won't use any band member's legal name without their permission and will use only approved photos. You can hire talent to design the merchandise; however, you must have the band's approval in order to actually make it. It's just the decent thing to do.

6. For the avoidance of doubt, we will own and have the perpetual right throughout the world to exploit the Artwork via any and all media, manner, configurations, transmissions, and devices known or hereafter devised. Your royalty for such exploitations will be fifty percent (50%) of our net profits.

This fifty-fifty split will continue forever in regard to any new merchandising ideas you and the artist come up with.

7. Artist may purchase any of our manufactured merchandise at any time, with a two-week notice, at wholesale cost, which varies depending on the product. Artist may then sell said merchandise for whatever price they see fit, the profit of which belongs solely to Artist.

Just as with CDs, the artist can purchase this merchandise at wholesale cost and sell it at shows for whatever markup they prefer, and then keep the profits for themselves.

In short, you have to protect yourself financially as the way music is bought and sold changes. The value of a CD may be changing, but T-shirts and other types of standard merchandise all have an intrinsic value that will not.

20

Management

The ultimate future of your record label might actually be to become an un-record label. Hear me out.

Rather than just putting out records and providing tour support for an artist, you might find that a label may better serve an artist by functioning as a management company on top of what you already do on a daily basis. This approach offers new ways to be supportive to an artist and also create new revenue streams. Providing management services might help you support artists while keeping your own shirt on your back.

Being a manager is a different role from running a record label, but the two roles can easily be intertwined. At the heart of the management profession is the simple goal of "taking care of things." A manager is the street-level person who is looking out for the artist's best interests at all times. A manager is the band's best friend who is willing to do—and good at doing—much, if not all, of the dirty work that comes with running a band.

The dirty work that comes with handling the mechanics of a struggling young band includes these tasks: managing the day-to-day logistics of who needs to be where and when; communicating between the band and the band's label; finding a label for the band if it doesn't have one; establishing connections with venues and booking agents; and constantly putting out feelers in the world to see if there are any unexplored opportunities for the band to dive into.

If a band is in its earliest stages, a manager could be a publicist, booking agent, attorney, and record label all wrapped up in one, based on the band's finances and necessity. A manager needs to promote the band constantly. If you don't have a publicist sending records and posters out to magazines, blogs, and venues, guess who's going to do it? If you can't find a booking agent to save your life for this band, guess who's going to put together the band's first northwest tour? The manager must fill in the gaps when the gaps appear, because there isn't someone there yet. In turn, while all this extra legwork is being done, it is also the manager's job to find other people to step into these roles eventually. A manager must always be connected to those elsewhere in the industry so that he or she can find the *right* publicist for the band, the *right* booking agent, and, hopefully, the *right*—or *any*—record label to help further the cause.

But with these large responsibilities comes a lot of upside. The manager wields a lot of power and influence. The manager steers the ship of the band and sets its direction. The manager also gets a cut of the band's collective revenue.

Below is a rough management agreement that will help get you started. An explanation follows each section:

MANAGEMENT AGREEMENT
This Agreement is made and entered into this ___ day of _____
_____, by and between [NAME OF COMPANY] (hereinafter "Company")
and [NAME OF ARTIST] (hereinafter "Artist"). Artist agrees to have
Company serve as his/her exclusive personal manager.

In consideration of the mutual covenants herein contained and other
good and valuable consideration, the parties agree as follows:
1. Obligations of Company. Company shall guide and advise Artist in
the music business. Company shall serve as Artist's exclusive agent
for the exploitation and promotion of Artist's music services and products throughout the world. Company shall work in association with

Artist in the negotiation of recording, merchandising, or other agreements affecting Artist's career throughout the Term of this Agreement.

This clause sets out the mission of a manager: to be the basis of trust for an artist as they experience the growing pains of finding their way through the music business. A manager must always be the reliable and responsible leader that looks out for the band—sort of a big brother or sister, that kind of vibe. A manager must fight the good fight on behalf of the band when negotiating record deals and merchandising agreements with labels and when dealing with the nitty-gritty aspects of running a business that the band doesn't want to—and shouldn't have to—deal with.

2. <u>The Term</u>. The Term of this Agreement shall continue for one (1) year after the date of execution of the agreement and may be renewed by mutual consent of the parties on the same terms for subsequent one-year terms.

This states that this management relationship will exist for one calendar year and can be renewed, based upon agreement between the band and manager at the end of the year. Furthermore, there will be some terms that will last longer than just the one year.

3. <u>Commission During the Term</u>. Company shall be entitled to _____ percent of Gross Revenues received by Artist during the Term. "Gross Revenues" shall be defined as all moneys including advances and fees received by Artist in connection with Artist's entertainment-related activities, but excluding: recording funds advanced by a record company; money paid to make videos; payments to record producers, musicians, mixers, remixers, directors, engineers, or any other individuals involved in the creation of audio or audiovisual recordings; payments to non–band member cowriters or copublishers; tour support; and any reimbursements received by Artist for expenses paid out of Gross Revenues.

All Gross Revenues shall be documented and reviewed and a compounded total shall be determined and mutually agreed upon by Artist and Company during the last week of each calendar month during the Term (no later than the twenty-eighth [28th] day of each calendar month), in which Company's commission shall be extracted.

In general, the commission for a full-time manager is anywhere from 10 to 12 percent of the gross revenue earned by the band; this includes everything the band makes, including money earned from shows, T-shirt sales, and CD sales. However, this doesn't include any sort of advance that may be provided by a record label or publishing company. The income for a manager comes in on a strictly peer-to-peer basis. Beyond that, this clause also stipulates that this commission will be paid to the manager at the end of every month.

4. Commissioning After the Term. Unless Company has been terminated for a breach of this Agreement, Company shall be entitled to postterm commission payments derived from master recordings released during the Term. Company shall not be entitled to income from albums released before or after the Term unless income earned from these albums is in compliance with a mutually agreed-upon alternative source or Company's commission and/or reimbursements. These postterm commission payments shall be at the following rates during the specific period:

10 percent of the Gross Revenues from the first six (6) month period after termination;

5 percent of the Gross Revenues from the second six (6) month period after termination;

3 percent of the Gross Revenues from the third six (6) month period after termination;

1 percent of the Gross Revenues from the fourth six (6) month period after termination;

Thereafter, Company shall receive no further postterm commissions.

All Gross Revenues shall be documented and reviewed and a compounded total shall be determined by Artist during the last week of each calendar month after the Term of this Agreement has expired (no later than the twenty-eighth [28th] day of each calendar month), in which Company's postterm commission shall be extracted until all postterm commission payment periods and percentages owed, first above listed, have expired.

Postterm payments may seem silly at first, but they really make a lot of sense. Building up a band is such a slow process and requires so much long-term planning that it would be hard to pinpoint when a manager's influence starts and stops. It may take months before there is any sort of dent made in the music market that can be attributed specifically to the manager's doing. On the other hand, the manager may luck out in his or her last week of work and score a big review in *Rolling Stone*, but then the very next week suddenly no longer be involved. This clause protects the manager's interest in that regard. The manager will see a steadily declining income as time goes on because the value of the manager's accomplishments will also decay over time. There isn't a magical switch that allows for the influence of one manager to shift to another, so this clause accounts for that.

5. <u>Company's Expenses</u>. Artist shall pay documented reasonable and necessary costs incurred by Company in connection with Company's duties on behalf of Artist. Artist shall pay such expenses only out of Gross Revenues commissionable under this Agreement unless Artist and Company mutually agree upon an alternative source to serve as Company's commissions and/or reimbursements in writing with the source clearly stated and defined. Artist shall not be personally liable for any such expenses. Company shall not incur expenses in excess of $200 in any single transaction, or $1,000 during any calendar month without Artist's prior written consent.

This clause dictates the manager's allowance. Everything that the manager buys on the artist's behalf must first be run by the artist for approval. If it all checks out, the money spent does not come from the artist's pocket, but from the revenue stream brought in by artist activities and sales. Therefore, the artist is not liable personally to pay back the manager for any expenses. The last line specifies that the manager cannot spend more than $1,000 a month and cannot spend more than $200 at one sitting without the artist's okay.

6. Mediation; Arbitration. If a dispute arises under this Agreement, the parties agree to first try to resolve the dispute with the help of a mutually agreed-upon mediator in the _____ county of _____. Any costs and fees other than attorney fees shall be shared equally by the parties. If it proves impossible to arrive at a mutually satisfactory situation, the parties agree to submit the dispute to binding arbitration in the _____ county of _____, conducted on a confidential basis pursuant to the Commercial Arbitration Rules of the American Arbitration Association.

If there is a disagreement between the artist and the manager, they must first try to settle the differences between them, but if that doesn't do the trick, then they must pick a state and county to settle the dispute with a professional arbitrator outside of court.

7. Ability to Perform. Artist certifies that it may enter into this Agreement and perform all its terms, and that the terms of this Agreement do not conflict with any other agreements of Artist. Artist agrees to hold Company harmless and indemnify Company for any damages, including, but not limited to, attorneys' fees and costs, incurred by Company in connection with any dispute over the ability of Artist to enter into this Agreement without violating the terms of another agreement.

This clause shows that the artist must be fully able to enter into the agreement and does not have any prior obligation to any other manager.

8. <u>Right to Consult Attorney</u>. All parties acknowledge that this is a legally binding contract; they have reviewed and understand its contents, and have had the opportunity to consult with an attorney of their choice.

It is always smart to run contracts like this by an attorney.

9. <u>General</u>. This Agreement may not be amended except in a writing signed by both parties. If a court finds any provisions of this Agreement invalid or unenforceable as applied to any circumstance, the remainder of this Agreement shall be interpreted so as best to effect the intent of the parties. This Agreement shall be governed by and interpreted in accordance with the laws of the State of _____. This Agreement expresses the complete understanding of the parties with respect to the subject matter and supersedes all prior proposals, agreements, representations, and understandings.

IN WITNESS WHEREOF, the parties hereto have read and executed this Agreement the day and year first above stated.

COMPANY
[NAME OF COMPANY]

_____

By: [NAME, TITLE]
ARTIST

_____

By: [NAME]

This agreement can be changed if both parties agree in writing on the outcome and future implications of that amendment.

To use movie ratings, this contract is a little PG, but it will get you through any initial bumps that you may run into when beginning to work with a growing artist. Management is certainly not a position that can be taken lightly. The band and everyone else who deals with it will have high expectations of you.

A management relationship is one of the most intimate forms of business that occurs in the music industry because a manager is involved in almost every facet of a band's existence. Don't head into such an agreement lightly. Think of it like moving in with a girlfriend or boyfriend; it means taking the relationship to a completely new level when neither party has been with the other before, so you need to be sure it is the right step to take.

If you are sure, then by all means take the plunge, because there is nothing more fun and more satisfying than helping a band grow from obscurity to stardom.

21

Licensing to Entertainment

Licensing is one of the best ways to make money in the music business, especially for a beginning label. It's crucial to consider the effects of licensing when entering into deals with artists.

Licensing refers to the process of selling someone the right to use one or many of the songs you have released. Just as my grandfather would go every May to purchase a license to go bass fishing for the summer, so must the producer of a television show, commercial, or film buy a license from you to put a song in a commercial, movie, or on a website.

Licensing also often corresponds with the terms *placement* or *synching*, which are labels most often heard around the indie-rock watercooler. Both describe the process of the placement of a piece of music or parts of a piece of music in a film, television show, or commercial. Every time you hear a little pop nugget being played during a car commercial, or hear a great song during some cinematic montage, the producers had to pay an artist and their label to use and license those songs.

In order to use and incorporate a song or part of another musical work in a broadcast event or film, producers must legally obtain the required licenses and consent from record companies, music publishers, and/or artists.

This is where the (perhaps unfamiliar) concept of getting paid real money comes in.

The price of a song license is relatively high even from small music labels, so this is something worth shooting for. That is, it's big for you, but little for a producer, making it a win-win situation. To a movie producer, spending $10,000 to $15,000 to license a song seems like a drop in the bucket, while for a small label it is a big freaking deal. This symbiotic relationship leaves both parties happy in the end.

So how do you make this connection? Just like everything else you do, the process begins when you send out a press kit and follow up on it. There are only a handful of placement companies in the country that will take on smaller indies like yours or mine, so you need to find them, befriend them, and send them good music.

In general, licensing can be a long and even arduous process that takes not weeks but months and maybe even more than a year. But it is completely worth the wait.

One of the great aspects of a licensing deal is that it can strike at any time and with any release you have ever put out. Although some films try to tap into what is popular at the moment to capture an immediate audience, most films try to incorporate timeless music that won't pigeonhole their work down the road. This means that any release in your current and back catalogs is fair game, which is just great. (Getting exposure from a website like Pitchfork may often prove to be difficult, because they limit their interest to your newest stuff, but you can promote a record for licensing deals for years until the right bite and the right fit come along, and you must take advantage of that.)

The Way Deals Work

Licensing deals can occur in a few different ways. You can license a single song to Target for a thirty-second commercial and get cut a single, one-time check for $5,000, or you can license a whole album to the Oxygen Network (Lifetime, WE channel) for long-term use that they will pay for through ASCAP or BMI, which I'll talk about a little later. Some deals, however, are founded on the term *en gratis*, which is French for "free" in the sense of "at no cost." Always be a little wary of these deals—the no-cost ones, that is. Not because people who want to use your music for free are shady, but because there may be some unforeseen circumstances involved. For instance, never agree to license a song to anyone en gratis if the deal isn't specific to a single event. If they want to use the song again for free, they need to talk to you again. Don't sign away any further rights to the song. Keep the deal focused and limited, because who knows when a song will take off?

The company that is purchasing the license must purchase "both sides" of the license. *Both sides* refers to the master itself (generally owned by the label) and the permission from the artist, which is the other "side."

Deals will come at you on different levels, which means you will enter into different agreements. If Sony Pictures Entertainment calls you asking to use "Oranges" by the Readers in a high-voltage action scene in their new *Batman* film, there will most definitely be a long contract and hopefully a large monetary sum involved. This is a situation in which you contact your lawyer, have him or her look over the deal and tell you what you are getting yourself into.

However, if a small independent filmmaker wants to put "Oranges" in a local film that will only ever be submitted to one film festival, you probably don't need to consult your lawyer. In fact, chances are that the filmmaker won't even have a contract to work with, so it may be just a spit-and-a-handshake type of contract that both parties draft together, or which you may even draft on your own. This can be a bit risky, so I recommend consulting a lawyer to draft a written agreement.

The aspect that truly distinguishes these two deals is scope. *Batman* will be shown in every theater in every country around the world. That results in the song's exposure to millions, not to mention the many more millions who will buy the film and hear the song again once it comes out on DVD and is released as part of the sound track on iTunes. The use of the song means two things: (a) you should definitely hold out for a lot of money, and (b) you should take into consideration the amount of exposure that the deal will provide for the song. Not only will Sony pay you up front, but the placement of this song in *Batman*, or in any major motion picture for that matter, will result in a vast runoff of residual sales that will also greatly benefit your release and your label.

When dealing with an independent filmmaker, you have to do a little research before agreeing to anything. The term *independent* is a wonderful label because it can describe anything from a small filmmaking company that actually makes real, let's-go-down-to-the-lobby-and-watch-an-indie-film films to the seventeen-year-old kid with a camcorder in his basement with blood capsules and cap guns.

It's great to have any sort of exposure in any number of avenues, but some opportunities carry more risks than others. And that is where you need to be vigilant. Work with people you trust, and use a lawyer any time it starts to feel like you're the one taking all the risks.

Another great arena for licensing is the video-game world. Increasingly, video games carry large and diverse sound tracks comprising songs by both established and new artists. For *Major League Baseball 2008*, Pitchfork served as the architect for the game's sound track—more evidence that video-game platforms are reaching out to bring in wider audiences, even through the music embedded in the game.

As your artists get a bit bigger and you find yourself getting consistent placements with each release, you might find that a synching company will approach you. This is a company that finds placement and synching opportunities on your behalf. These deals are generally pretty straightforward, with a 20 percent commission taken by the company from both sides. It seems like a lot (because it is), but these companies will be going after big money that you might not normally have access to, so they are often well worth the high commission.

Shared Copyright

Generally in independent deals—and specifically in the contract I outline above—you share the copyright with your artists. This means that not only do you split any profits from a licensing deal, but also you must receive permission from the artist involved before proceeding with a deal. If you own 50 percent of the song, then you surely do not own all of it, so you obviously cannot offer 100 percent of the permission required to sell the license—you can offer only 50 percent.

Most licensing deals are clear-cut and worth the commitment required. Still, an artist may have an opinion—you are selling the results of their creative process—so remember to always ask, and ask nicely!

BMI and ASCAP

BMI and ASCAP are performance rights organizations, also known as PROs. Their whole existence revolves around accountability. Their job is to collect royalties on behalf of musicians for the "performance" of their copyrighted material. *Performance* is the key word. It means that every time a song by one of your artists is played on the radio, played at a hockey game, or featured in a commercial (and every time their video is played on MTV), BMI or ASCAP collects royalties from the producers, radio stations, and companies who play the song in a public setting. Once they collect the royalty, they take a commission and then pay the artist or publishing company.

BMI and ASCAP each collect royalties in their own way, and it is absolutely crucial that *all* your artists be registered with one of these companies.

I have tried to imagine a world without PROs. The best scenario I can picture is a world plunged into darkness and chaos. Honestly, all I can think of is the opening scene of *Monty Python's The Meaning of Life*, in which two office buildings sail past each other like pirate ships and all the office workers use filing cabinets as cannons to engage in mortal combat. Seriously, it wouldn't be good. Imagine if every single radio station in the world—of which there are a great many—had to pay the owner of every song directly. Radio stations would barely function. On planet Earth, there is a nearly infinite number of musicians and recorded works and the number is growing constantly. Thanks to BMI and ASCAP, the potentially insane process of managing performance rights is somewhat manageable.

A solicitor general's brief, submitted to the U.S. Supreme Court in 1967, stated this in regards to PROs:

> A central licensing agency such as ASCAP is the only practical way that copyright proprietors may enjoy their rights under the federal copyright laws and that broadcasters and others may conveniently obtain licenses for the performance of copyrighted music. We found that single copyright owners cannot deal individually with all users or individually police the use of their songs; and that a single radio station may broadcast as many as 60,000 performances of musical compositions involving as many as 6,000 separate compositions.

The word *police* is revealing here. Without PROs, labels like ours would have to listen to every single radio station that could possibly be playing our music at all times to determine whether or not something of ours is being aired. Furthermore, if and when one of our songs was played, then we would have to bill the radio station.

Beyond that, we would have to make sure we got paid for that performance and we really wouldn't have much power to enforce such requests.

The amount of work committed to the task of policing performance rights is staggering. Employees of both ASCAP and BMI listen to 400,000 hours of radio a year and analyze the music used in television for roughly six million hours. Do you have the time for that? No, and I don't either.

A Little Background

ASCAP was founded in 1914 and was the first full-service publishing rights organization. ASCAP claims to have the oldest and largest catalog in the United States and adds roughly 100,000 new titles every year. However, ASCAP represents only 150,000 artists and publishers, whereas BMI actually supports more.

ASCAP gets paid by issuing a "blanket license" to use its entire catalog to radio and television stations, after which they adjust according to the results of their research into what is being played.

BMI was founded in 1940 as a direct challenge in competition with ASCAP and to give writers who were rejected by ASCAP representation, support, and a voice. Representing nearly 300,000 artists and publishers, BMI's catalog includes some 4.5 million works. BMI also operates under a "blanket license" system and charges broadcasters a fee based on adjustment formulas offset against gross receipts.

Relying on statistical sampling, both BMI and ASCAP have elaborate methods of tracking radio airplay and number of performances. For television reporting, however, ASCAP and BMI both count the number of performances rather than using statistical sampling methods. Furthermore, both companies record and tape network television performances to double-check the reports given by networks and television producers.

I wish everything could be tabulated in this fashion: good old-fashioned counting. But it's just not realistic. Using statistical sampling methods, ASCAP and BMI can project the frequency of play on local radio stations. It is something of a mystery exactly what formulas and what methods of statistical analysis they use, but both companies assure us that "samples are multiplied by formulas established by leading statisticians who are selected separately by each organization." Both methods represent fair sampling and both are technically equally accurate.

When dealing with sampling specifically, both companies weight the samples they analyze according to the size of each radio or television station's audience, using a model much like the CMJ weighting system that governs college radio airplay.

In terms of payment, ASCAP functions under the "current performance plan," which is based on the number of performances (or "credits") recorded by ASCAP's tracking system. Each credit is worth a certain amount based upon the number of blanket licenses purchased that year. In 2003, it was $5.67 per credit. So if one of your artists was played once on a Top 40 radio station, ASCAP would know that and then pay you a royalty based on the value of that one credit. However, some performances are worth more credits than others, depending on when and in which market the song was played.

As for BMI, their payment methods are a little less clear-cut. BMI asks us to accept that payments are made "in accordance with the current practices and rates of BMI," which it says are "similar to [those] of other performing rights organizations throughout the world." Well, that's a relief.

Both companies are very good about updating their policies on their respective official websites.

22

Saying No to Friends

The founders of young labels often ask me, "At what level of success is a label able to say no to its friends' bands?"

You can start saying no to our friends' bands simply whenever you are able to. Yes, that does sound like a cop-out answer, because it is. I liken this to knowing when a band needs a manager. If they miss a flight because they have a double-booked meeting and also slept in, sounds like the band needs a manager. In order to get your new label off the ground, you have to embrace your friends first, because they will be the first people in line ready to trust you with their near and dear musical efforts. However, you will get to the point of no longer needing—or wanting—to release your friends' records. That point comes when all your time and money resources are being used by artists who produce revenues and when your friends' bands do not.

Spending a few years in "friend mode" really isn't all that bad. The advantages include that, because your friends are your friends, they'll be patient (more or less) while you fumble your way through running your label. They'll come to your shows, they'll blog on your behalf, they'll buy your T-shirts. You need that sort of forgivingness and loyalty as you make mistakes and grow up through your record-label business infancy.

Another perk is that communicating with friends is often easier than with strangers. Friends are around a lot, they get you, you get them. Count your blessings before you try to grow out of them too quickly. It may be a situation similar to realizing how sweet you had it in college before you had to get a real job, or how sweet you had it in elementary school—because elementary school was just that sweet.

So how do you know when the hour has come to cut the friend cord? This is often the point at which many label folks claim they became—or never became—a "real" record label. A good way to measure this is to keep track of a band you fancy that is a bit bigger than your label. Once your label gets to the point where you can imagine approaching that band with some credibility, you are in the position to go it alone. Hopefully not friendless but friends-as-clients-less.

I sized up Afternoon Records at several stages, by looking at a few different bands. When I first started the label, I tried to grow at a rate that would allow me to sign two great local Minneapolis bands called the Cardinal Sin and the Plastic Constellations. Both were excellent bands that I had followed closely since high school. They were each always out of my reach: the Cardinal Sin, sadly, broke up about six months before I got to the point of being ready for them, and the Plastic Constellations signed to Brooklyn-based indie tastemakers Frenchkiss Records. After that breakup and the Plastic Constellations' moving to a larger label, I measured Afternoon Records against So Many Dynamos and Someone Still Loves You Boris Yeltsin, bands that toured extensively, received good reviews, and already had interest from other labels. But then they both signed to bigger labels than mine. The cycle continues.

Here is a more concrete answer to the question at the top of this chapter: if you are financially independent, if you are not supporting the label out of your own pocket, if you have great distribution, if Pitchfork, *Spin*, and *Rolling Stone* all know who you are and care at least a teensy bit about you, and if you can send a band out on tour for more than thirty days at a stint—then you are ready to leave your kind friends' bands behind and embrace the music and talent of total strangers.

23

Odds and Ends

For those subjects that haven't been sorted easily into one category or another, here is a bit of a hodgepodge of tips.

CDs and Bands

When you make a record, after all is said and done, how do you settle up with a band so that they can have some CDs to sell at shows and on tour? This can be a complex situation. Depending on both the size of the label and the distance between the band and the label's headquarters, you can deal with this in a few different ways.

For the first four or so years of running Afternoon Records, I gave bands records to sell at shows based on the honor system. I gave them CDs when they asked for them; they sold them at shows, kept track of how many they sold, and then, at the end of the month, sent a check to the label for its cut of what was sold. This worked great for the most part, and I ran into only a few snafus here and there. It's a good model if all the bands on your label are from the same geographic area. In my case, I was close friends with all the bands on my label and saw each band on a regular basis. That proximity helped keep the honor system honorable.

To make this particular method work, this is what you have to do. Let's say that the Readers give you a call, wanting to pick up a new batch of CDs. You first have to determine how many CDs constitute a batch. I suggest a hundred; it's easy to carry and count out that many, and that's also the amount that generally comes in boxes from distributors.

You will hand out only one batch at a time to a band. If they need more CDs, they must have already sold that previous hundred and paid you your cut for them. Looking at your ledger, you should be able to determine if all those CDs are accounted for. If they are, you can hand out the next batch. If not, ask the band what happened to the absent CDs. When they come to pick up the new batch or when you send out a batch to them, you must keep a ledger for CDs that have been signed out. In fact, it often helps to just have a chart on a clipboard and have the band sign out each batch with a signature, a date, and a quantity all noted, so that everyone is on the same page.

However, as my label got bigger and the bands I worked with were eventually based all over the country, I decided to adopt a different approach in a few special cases. In fact, most labels adopt the following method: charge the band for the CDs at distribution cost and then let the band sell them for whatever they like at shows and keep the profit for themselves.

Now, instead of giving even my own band, One for the Team, a hundred CDs and expecting the band to pay Afternoon Records back for them once they have sold, I sell the band each batch of CDs at distribution cost (the fee that distributors pay for the CD), which is generally about $6 or $7. Then, the band can sell those CDs at shows for $10 or $12 and keep the rest as profit. My label gets all its money in one sale.

With this method, you don't have to track down record sales from the band, and you can save a lot of time trying to balance schedules and also align accounting books between the band and the label.

I also believe that both the label and the band benefit from the purchasing of the CDs, rather than the consigning of them. The label gets a nice sum of money up front for each exchange and the band gets to keep the profits from the sale of each unit.

An Online Presence

Building a grassroots following online is almost as important as building one in real life, because the two can—and most likely will—grow into the same thing. You can take a small local band and turn it into a national or international product online without touring or exorbitant spending.

With a functional website and ambitious MySpace presence, you can bridge the gap between inactive and active with only a few hours of commitment a week.

MySpace is exciting. It offers an easy-to-use way to promote your bands and connect directly with your audience and fans. That is absolutely priceless. Your bands will have to be genuinely good in order to get anyone on MySpace to care about them, but if you can provide the opportunity for listeners to form an opinion about your music when they formerly didn't know about your label, then you've accomplished something valuable.

On MySpace, keep things interesting. Update frequently and change things around a bit. Feel free to represent yourself and your bands in their own way. Use this as an opportunity to project an image that coincides with your goals.

On your label's own website, you have to one-up MySpace. You need to provide more content, more pics, more videos, and more opportunities for fun and simple ways for fans to interact with your bands—and you.

You need to have a spot for your curious visitors to listen to MP3s, see pictures, view videos, and, most important, buy stuff.

Organization

Organization is the single greatest asset to any business owner, and in the music industry, it's essential. Here's where the pros separate from the hacks. Make lists. Keep records. Get organized.

When there is so much to do and so little time to do it in,

time management and multitasking are key skills to acquire and develop.

When I first started dipping my toe into the pool of indie-rock record releasing, I had no idea what was actually involved in putting out a record. So diving in like a fool, I made many, many mistakes, all of which could have been prevented—or at least minimized— by simple organizational tools and mechanisms. I've learned. Now I'm teaching you.

The first big lesson of organization is to put everything in writing. When it comes to important conversations and deals with bands and prospective clients, it is crucial to know what was said (exactly) and to have the ability to quickly access notes on the conversation. So I must encourage the constant use of e-mail and the diligent saving of notes on all important conversations. Should there be any future confusion, you'll have a record of the original agreement to clear it up, so both parties can move on.

The key to any good organizational workspace is the almighty and powerful list. Oh yes, I love lists. Before work every morning— and sometimes before bed the evening prior—I make extensive lists outlining exactly what it is I need to accomplish that or the next day. Okay, so there is a certain element of OCD going on with that. Still, it really does help set priorities and pace your day.

Staying in the Know

Stay in the know. For as long as you can, as best you can, you need to keep your ears to the ground and know the goings-on around town in the local music scene and in the national independent music gossip circuit.

Scenesters love to gossip, so this isn't as hard to do as you might think. The best way to keep on your toes and up on the most current events in the music industry is to subscribe to a handful of music magazines and read another handful of blogs every day.

The music magazines that still prove to be reliable sources of interesting trend-based industry information are *Billboard*, *CMJ New Music Monthly*, *Paste*, *MAGNET*, and *Rolling Stone*.

When it comes to the big magazines, the news is accurate, but it is usually a little late and a little bit watered down compared to online sources. Still, you gotta know at least that much.

Supplementing news from larger sources with blogs is the way to go. But you must stay on top of the always changing popularity and reliability of blogs. Pitchfork, Stereogum, Pop Matters, and Brooklyn Vegan are all daily online music sources that don't seem to be going away anytime soon. If something interesting is going on in the music world, they know about it first and are spreading the word. Make sure you're subscribing.

Priorities

I never forget who I work for: the artists on my label. When they call, I answer; when they need help, I help them; and when they need attention, I give it to them. That's probably one of the biggest things I have to sell: my accessibility. If an artist needs help and it's not an unreasonable hour and not my significant other's birthday, I chat, I e-mail, I talk, I go. I want them to feel appreciated, because I do appreciate them. It isn't phony. I'm here because of them.

I'm not a slave to my artists, but I love them, I love the music, and I love the business. When I can help a band become a little bit better or boost their revenues—and mine—a little bit, that's a good day for me.

And I hope those get to be good days for you, too.